AF484966

# BOXING THE OCTOPUS

# BOXING THE OCTOPUS

**JONI RODGERS**

*NEW YORK TIMES BESTSELLING AUTHOR*

*Boxing the Octopus: The Worst Way to Become an Almost Famous Author and the Best Advice I Got While Doing It*

© 2022 Joni Rodgers

All rights reserved. No part of this publication may be reproduced in any form or by any electronic or mechanical means, including information storage and retrieval systems, without permission in writing by the publisher, except by a reviewer who may quote brief passages in a review. For information regarding permission, contact the publisher.

Published by Westport Lighthouse Books

jonirodgers.com

Westport, WA

Library of Congress Control Number: 2022900665

Paperback ISBN: 979-8-9855494-9-2

Ebook ISBN: 979-8-9855495-0-8

Cover design by Kapo Ng

Interior design by Liz Schreiter

Edited and produced by Reading List Editorial

ReadingListEditorial.com

Publisher's Cataloging-in-Publication Data

Names: Rodgers, Joni.

Title: Boxing the octopus : the worst way to become an almost famous author and the best advice I got while doing it / Joni Rodgers.

Description: Westport, WA : Westport Lighthouse Books, 2022. | Previously published as First You Write. | Summary: Author of the bestselling memoir Bald in the Land of Big Hair, Joni Rodgers shares words of wisdom for aspiring writers and her opinions on where the publishing industry is headed.

Identifiers: LCCN 2022900665 | ISBN 9798985549492 (pbk.) | ISBN 9798985549508 (ebook)

Subjects: LCSH: Authorship -- Handbooks, manuals, etc.| Creative writing. | Self-publishing -- Handbooks, manuals, etc. | BISAC: LANGUAGE ARTS & DISCIPLINES / Publishers & Publishing Industry.| LANGUAGE ARTS & DISCIPLINES / Writing / Authorship. | LANGUAGE ARTS & DISCIPLINES / Writing / Business Aspects.

Classification: LCC PN147.R63 2022 | DDC 808.02 R63 2022—dc23

LC record available at https://lccn.loc.gov/2022900665

# Contents

# IT'S A GREAT LIFE, IF YOU DON'T WEAKEN.

Sir John Buchan

AUTHOR OF *THE THIRTY-NINE STEPS*

# INTRODUCTION

We are living in the most thrilling publishing era since Gutenberg. In February 2012, I wrote a condensed prototype of this book on my MacBook Air during a flight from Houston to Brussels. While I visited the Magritte museum, ate strange cheeses, and slept for a few hours in Belgium, two members of the Midwives, my critique group, read the draft and made notes. The next day, I input their edits while I rode the bullet train from Brussels to St. Pancras Station in London. Drinking coffee in the kitchen of Irish author Orna Ross—whom I'd seen many times on Facebook and Skype but met for the first time that morning at the Willesden Green tube station—I used Scrivener to convert the manuscript to ebook format and assigned it an ISBN from the spares I keep on hand. That evening, sitting in the Espresso Corner at Earls Court with the London Book Fair in full swing all around me, I uploaded the file with a cover I designed myself, because the one I paid to have designed a few weeks earlier didn't float my boat. The following morning, while I participated in a panel on established authors going indie, the book titled *First You Write* went live on Amazon, and audience members were able to scan a QR code from my business card to download it for free. While I waited in line for a glass of wine that afternoon, two people popped over to tell me they'd already read it.

It was a quick read—and still is. I promise. The point of this exercise was to illustrate how mind-blowingly fast things were moving in the industry at the time. The point of telling you about it now is to illustrate how mind-blowingly fast the industry continues to evolve. Ten seconds after I pulled the trigger on that ebook, the fresh technology was old hat. Conversations about publishing tech need to take place in real time. We're talking about writing here. The art and act of transmuting thought and emotion to language transcends technology. It is what it is on stone, papyri, Moleskine notebook, dot matrix, digital, and whatever comes next. Trying to make heads or tails of the publishing industry will suck your head inside out and, if you have any sense of justice, break your heart. If you're going to be pragmatic about it, when you feel the urge to put your words out into the world, you should run—*run*—the other way.

Kristin Chenoweth tells her Broadway Boot Camp students: "If there's anything else you can do for a living and still be happy, do it." I urge the same caution on aspiring writers. It's hard work, if you're doing it right, and the joy of doing that work is sometimes difficult to hold onto, because it's done mostly in solitude, without reward.

If you're trying to learn how to be a writer, there's limited net gain in studying some other writer's *Lord of the Rings* journey in minute detail—the angst of the draft, the vagaries of critical butt-fluffers— because the environment is constantly changing and every writer's journey is unique. There's no step-by-step IKEA construction manual to follow, because art should be undisciplined. Craft is where discipline comes in.

## IN THE ART OF WRITING, THERE ARE NO RULES, ONLY REASONS.

Let's not even pretend this little book is about to teach you what to write or how to publish or anything else you don't already know. No one can tell you how to intuit your art, practice your craft, or run your business. I can only tell you what's worked (or not) for me and perhaps offer a few general pirate rules, which are "more like guidelines," as Johnny Depp reminds us in *Pirates of the Caribbean*. Prefacing with a big fat FWIW, I'll offer a few encouraging suggestions that might point you in a direction you haven't thought of or clarify a direction you have thought of. Perhaps it's a direction you've always yearned toward from the corner of your eye while the world, your loved ones, and other satanic forces united to convince you that your notion of being a writer was adorable but insane. I can tell you: *I've been there*. I can't tell you it will get easier.

This is the not necessarily chronological, occasionally metaphorical, but pretty much exactly true story of how I made it onto the *New York Times* bestseller list. And it's the story of why that didn't matter as much as I thought it would. I'm throwing in tidbits of wisdom I started collecting in a little desk caddy before I actually had a desk to put it on. I've also asked several of my writer friends, including the Midwives and other colleagues, to contribute 100ish words of advice on craft and writing life.

That's essentially my education as a writer: reading, seeking, asking questions, and recognizing that I still have a lot to learn. Any pearls of wisdom here were given to me as gifts; I've figured out very little on my own. My education as an editor comes from decades of being stringently, mercilessly edited by some of the best in the biz.

## THE ONLY WAY TO GROW AS A WRITER IS TO WRITE.

So there's room in these pages for you to add your own words. I'll challenge you to get past the decision fatigue of everyday existence and prompt some self-querying, but as I see it, all white space is fair game as we put up our dukes and take on this many-tentacled beast that is the writing life.

LET ME LIVE, LOVE, AND SAY
IT WELL IN GOOD SENTENCES.

SYLVIA PLATH
AUTHOR OF THE BELL JAR

# GO FORTH

Anyone attempting to make a living and a life in the arts must reinvent their own wheel. One stellar example of that early in my career was the late, great Rue McClanahan. While I was working with Rue, ghostwriting her memoir and subsequently adapting it for a one-woman show, we had many long conversations about what it means to be an artist.

Most people remember Rue as Blanche Devereaux on *The Golden Girls*, but that role was a small part of her long, impressive acting career, and acting was only one facet of her life as an artist. Rue took ballet from early childhood and studied at Jacob's Pillow as a teen. She was a drama major at the University of Tulsa and studied acting with Uta Hagen at the Berghof Studio in New York, where she learned about a level of specificity and intention that can and must apply to good writing:

## "YOU MUST LEARN TO COMMUNICATE VOLUMES WITH AN EYELASH."

She wanted to be taken seriously as an actress but knew her greatest gift was that she was funny as hell—on stage, on camera, and in real life. At the time Rue's memoir was published, there was a *Golden Girls* rerun playing somewhere in the world every hour of every day. She embraced Blanche, but it's not how she wanted to be remembered. She wanted her book to be funny—that was a given—but Rue also wanted to say something meaningful about life and art. She hoped her son, a jazz guitarist, would read this book and understand a few things about his own life as an artist.

Rue's early hardscrabble gigs included everything from singing waitress to angsty film noir. One night in the early 1950s, she bent to light a gas stove and was blown back against a wall, horribly burned. Two days later, in searing pain, thick body makeup covering her peeling skin, she shot a semi-nude love scene for *Walk the Angry Beach* (later released as *Hollywood After Dark*.) She agonized over long periods away from her son, lived out of suitcases and closets, sacrificed anything and everything she had to, not to be rich or famous, but to practice her craft.

Rue's joy, generosity, and capacity for love were childlike and unstoppable. She painted and did wildly colorful ink graphics that cluttered the walls of her eclectic Manhattan apartment. She designed and constructed her own costumes early on and didn't hesitate to offer input when she later had the luxury of designers crafting clothes for her.

She also wrote. And wrote. And wrote.

She'd dabbled with short stories since she was young and in the 1970s collaborated with a friend on an off-off-Broadway musical called *Oedipus Schmedipus, As Long as You Love Your Mother*. When I was brought in by Random House to help Rue with her memoir, she handed me a walloping 800 or so pages of material she'd already produced under the title *My First Five Husbands*. Our main challenge: Rue never met a billboard, song lyric, stray dog, walnut shell, math problem, taxi driver, or English muffin that didn't have some hilariously epic story attached to it. Everything fascinated her. She read books about philosophy and physics—yes, Blanche fans, physics!—and history.

Structurally, the thing was an incomprehensible M. C. Escher staircase to oblivion, but the writing itself was very good. Rue was extremely smart and incredibly funny. I waded through the whole hilariously brilliant quagmire, making copious notes and plotting a possible course for the manuscript that would skim a lot of foam from the prose but still keep Rue's adventures and distinctive voice intact. Then I returned to New York, and after dinner and a walk up the street for cigarettes, we sat out on her patio with the behemoth manuscript and a bottle of red wine between us.

"You don't need a ghostwriter," I told her. "You need a book doctor."

"I don't like that term," she said. "My book is not sick. It's healthy. Like a Sumo wrestler."

I quoted Fred Ramey, the editor of my first novel:

## "THERE'S A DIFFERENCE BETWEEN A BOOK AND 800 PAGES OF GOOD WRITING."

"I'm listening," Rue said warily.

"First, we have to decide what this book is about," I said. "Then we have to figure out what it's *really* about."

This is never the no-brainer it seems to be at first blush. Obviously, Rue's extraordinary life was an entertaining series of events, but you can tell any story in a variety of ways. This story I'm telling you now, for example, covers some of the same events I covered in my memoir *Bald in the Land of Big Hair*, but that book was about my family's difficult journey through the valley of cancer and recovery, and this little book is about becoming a writer. Very different perspective. And perspective is everything when it comes to storytelling. Ask Isaac and Ishmael.

"What do you see as a central theme in your life story?" I asked Rue.

She raised one brow and answered in a practiced whiskey alto:

## "DON'T TRY THIS AT HOME."

We laughed, because her exploits and sexploits were not for the faint-hearted, but to me, that really did nutshell the way she lived her artistic life. I suggested to her that perhaps, as an artist, it's not possible for one to accomplish anything truly self-willed and free of inhibition from within the snuggly confines of home, and by "home"

I mean your comfort zone, wherever that may be, even if it's an imaginary place where everyone loves you unconditionally, and you feel oh-so-sugar-cookie-right with the world. If we harbor any hope of growing, evolving, or making a difference, we must leap from that cozy nest and put ourselves out into the cold, cruel unknown.

Rue pondered all that for the duration of a long, contemplative drag on her cigarette.

"I'm taking off my pants," she said.

"Excuse me?"

"These pants. They're terribly uncomfortable." Rue shucked out of her double-knit trousers. She was wearing a gauzy thigh-length tunic blouse, so this was an unexpected but not completely loony thing to do. She propped her pale legs up in the sunshine, contemplating.

"You're a preacher," said Rue.

"I hope not," I said, "but I do believe in the power of the parable. The way Jesus and Buddha used stories. That's what makes memoirs worth writing. We each have a tiny fragment of the map of human experience."

## SHARING OUR STORIES, WE CONTRIBUTE TO THE COSMIC CARTOGRAPHY.

I didn't know that's what I was doing when I wrote *Bald in the Land of Big Hair*, but during the first two years after it was published by HarperCollins, thousands of letters from readers quickly educated me. I wrote that book because I needed to process this huge thing that had happened to me: an aggressive course of chemotherapy for blood cancer. Writing is how I process things. I hoped the general audience would be entertained and that other women with cancer would feel a little less isolated; I didn't expect people to filter my story through their own struggles—divorce, bereavement, loss, everyday frustration—and arrive at a meaning I had no part in engineering.

But of course, they did. That's what readers do.

As a reader, that's what I would have done. That's what I *have* done thousands of times as a reader. Trying to control that dynamic as a writer is futile, because I can't keep the reading experience confined to my own patio. I don't have the opportunity to justify my creative choices, explain my motives, or make excuses for my errors. Once the book is out there, it has a life of its own, with an energy and direction largely deployed by readers, and a chunk of my naked soul is going to be out there with it. That's the simultaneously terrifying and exhilarating truth of what it means to be published.

Midwife Barbara "Bobbi" Taylor Sissel:

> ## "SOMETIMES, WHAT THE READERS GET OUT OF THE STORY IS SO UNEXPECTED, IT TAKES YOUR BREATH AWAY."

One of the first books I read in the wake of my cancer diagnosis was Betty Rollin's iconic breast cancer memoir, *First You Cry*. I was just trying to get some nebulous idea of what the hell was happening to me, but the story took me way beyond that to an examination of what it means to be a woman and a writer. In her foreword to the twenty-fifth anniversary edition of *First You Cry*, Rollin talks about how terrifying it was to put herself out there like that "because in 1975, you didn't blab about yourself the way everyone does today. Blabbing on paper helped me. It tidied up the mess that was inside my head. When it was done, I felt right-side-up again." She describes that book as "a selfish act for which I keep getting thanked."

In my humble opinion, that's what every book should be. Memoir or fiction, it should ring true. It should cost you something to write, but the writing should pay you back with insights, private laughs, and the satisfaction of getting something ugly out of your system or solidifying something dear at a fixed point in your heart. Writing should be about your experience, not the reader's; we'll take care of them in the editing phase. The writing of a book should be entirely about private creative joy and the unexpected gifts that have nothing to do with publication, sales, or critical acceptance.

## IT SHOULD BE A PERILOUS JOURNEY.

"And it should be performed with love," Bobbi gently reminds me.

Only you know what your next step should be, and yes, you do know.

You know.

Don't sit there saying you don't know, when the truth is you do, but no one has validated it for you yet.

Newsflash: *No one is coming to validate it for you.*

If they do, you won't believe them, so let that go. Set a rat trap in your head and snap the spine of that sneaky, gnawing need for validation.

You know how to write. You've gotten very good at setting words cleverly in rows. And you know that you have something to say, a story to tell, a parable to share.

Don't try this at home.

Go out on a limb and try it where the winds of conscience and inspiration are blowing. Try it from the perspective of a character's eye and a reader's head, testing your psychic powers of empathy and imagination. Try it on a train across the border into the Nazi territory of public criticism, with all your self-doubt and second-guessing stuffed under your hat and all the gifts you know you have to offer sewn into the lining of your coat.

Two weeks before Rue died, I sat with her at the patio table in her sunny little backyard on Manhattan's upper east side. A lifelong dancer, voracious reader, uninhibited artist, and deliciously garrulous conversation maker, she'd been fighting hard to regain her mobility and speech since suffering a stroke a few months earlier. Her eyes were bright, full of things she wanted to say, but every syllable was an act of will. It took a long time to ask if I wanted lunch, even longer to fill me in on "all the drama."

She thanked me for not jumping in to finish sentences. People kept doing that without knowing the specific word she was grappling with. They'd interject "lucky," she told me, where she'd say "serendipitous," and she forged that word—serendipitous—with the painstaking tenacity of a glassblower. Words were important to Rue.

Listen to what Frank Capra, director of *It's a Wonderful Life*, said about specificity and intention:

## "DO NOT COMPROMISE. BELIEVE IN YOURSELF. ONLY THE VALIANT CAN CREATE."

Writing is an act of courage from beginning to end, and you may find that the words soar highest when you feel most fragile and afraid. Whatever you fear—failure, criticism, resounding quiet—embrace it. Make it work for you.

Go forth and write.

Be valiant. Be a creator. Be you.

NO WRITING IS A WASTE OF TIME—NO CREATIVE WORK WHERE THE FEELINGS, THE IMAGINATION, THE INTELLIGENCE MUST WORK.

BRENDA UELAND
AUTHOR OF *IF YOU WANT TO WRITE: A BOOK ABOUT ART, INDEPENDENCE AND SPIRIT*

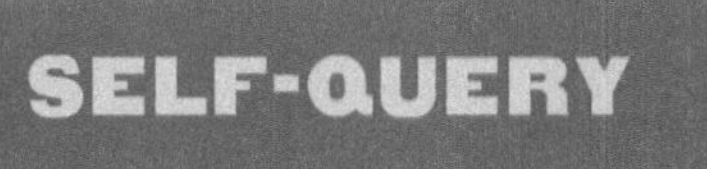



# WHAT'S MY STORY?

Thinking about your story—the story of your own life or the story you're trying to tell—ask yourself:

Where does it begin?

_______________________________________________

_______________________________________________

_______________________________________________

_______________________________________________

How does it end?

_______________________________________________

_______________________________________________

_______________________________________________

_______________________________________________

Identify three priorities that shape the story:

_______________________________________________

_______________________________________________

_______________________________________________

_______________________________________________

**BE BRAVE. LOOK THE WRITING IN THE EYE AND DON'T FLINCH. MAKE IT STRONGER. IT WOULD BE SO MUCH EASIER TO DO SOMETHING ELSE, GIVE UP, GO OFF, BUT IF YOU DO, YOU'LL NEVER TOUCH THE STORY THAT IS WAITING, THAT IS ASKING FOR YOU, RIGHT THERE AT YOUR ELBOW. SET CHIN. LINK ARMS. BEND YOUR KNEES. WORK.**

DR. MYLÈNE DRESSLER
AUTHOR OF *THE LAST TO SEE ME*

# 2

# ROLL WITH THE CHANGES

Technically, this is my second go-round as an indie author. My first foray into self-publishing was back in 1975. I was an eighth-grade misfit at an academically boffo but ideologically stifling Evangelical Lutheran school in LaCrosse, Wisconsin.

Even before I broke into an ungainly growth spurt that left me a head taller than every boy in my class, I was an unpretty girl with hand-me-down clothes and a humidity-activated frizz-bush of reddish-brown hair, which I attempted to curl on orange juice cans or straighten with the clothes iron, my head mashed down against the ironing board.

A sheltered, small-town nerd from a conservative Christian family, I'd never been kissed and wasn't allowed to see PG-rated movies, but I'd been secretly gorging myself on a book-a-day diet of romance novels for about a year. Not the slim category romance novels, mind you; these were chunky Gothics and historicals: Taylor Caldwell, Barbara Taylor Bradford, the Kent Family Chronicles by John Jakes, anything and everything by Kathleen E. Woodiwiss. I read constantly—rabidly, on the weekends—and I read fast, consuming the pages like a woodchipper.

Most of these books found their way into circulation through three or four mothers of my classmates, and one of these moms subscribed to the old *True Confessions Magazine*. Every issue was immediately pilfered, passed around and read ragged before the love-starved mom ever saw it. The stories were typically titled "My Boyfriend Joined the Navy" or "A Sophomore's Secret" or some such. I was smart enough to sense that the stories were stupid, patriarchal, and the opposite of politically correct. They were prurient drivel, and we loved them. I was so ill-informed about the facts of life that, for me, they were a crash course in anatomy and an epic miseducation in everything else. There seemed to be some indication that a man's "root" underwent some sort of measurable transformation when "pulsing" against a woman's "center"? WTF!

Post Chatterley, but pre-Google, I was intrigued.

Since I was also reading Austen, du Maurier, and the Sisters Brontë, it didn't take long for me to recognize that the craftwork in *True Confessions* was not all that complicated. I noodled out a few florid trifles featuring television characters in the type of story that would later be called "fan fiction"—like the Twilight-inspired erotica that spawned *Fifty Shades of Grey.* John Boy Walton loses his virginity to a woman selling encyclopedias door to door. Rhoda and Mary move to Paris where their Sapphic love is less misunderstood. The Roman characters on *I, Claudius* engage in all manner of kinky escapades, which, looking back on it, was probably nothing compared to the kinky shit they did in real life.

The other girls in my class were mightily entertained and encouraged me to do more. Because I knew virtually nothing about sex beyond the fanciful "pulsing" and "engorging" alluded to in *True Confessions* and the "manroot" physiology of my romance novel tutelage, my stories relied heavily on witty banter and lush descriptions of locations, current pop music, and fast food.

One day in a fit of eighth-grade pique, I wrote a story about one of the mean girls in my class getting it on with a galactically uncool boy she professed to despise. I didn't mean for it to make the rounds and certainly didn't mean for it to get back to the mean girl, but it did, of course, and she loved it. She offered me a dollar for it.

Just like that, I was in the writing business.

For a dollar a page, I would customize a brief romance story starring my classmate "client" and her made-to-order crush. In cases where the real-life crush failed to live up to expectations, a brief epilogue featuring his untimely death could be had for a quarter. One Friday night, I was sailing around the roller rink—not in the center with the slow-dancers, out at the perimeter with the other undatables—when a girl I didn't know skimmed over to me and said, "Are you the one who writes stories?"

"Um…"

I blinked, wide-eyed, thinking I was about to be punched in the face or reported to the principal. But now I look back and love that girl. She was the first person who invited me to embrace this simple truth about myself, a simple truth I need to be reminded of whenever I get sucked into the blah blah blah of publishing and platforming:

## I AM THE ONE WHO WRITES STORIES.

"Can you write one about me and him?" she asked, nodding toward a boy who was slow-dance skating with someone else.

The tear-jerking love triangle was unspooling in my head before I could even form the word "Yes!" I would have written it, dollar or not. And that's the frisson of *yes!* I feel around for in every ghostwriting gig I take on today.

Word spread, and I expanded my customer base, passing off the folded pages in the privacy of the grimy girls' bathroom like a drug dealer. It was nice to have a few dollars of my own. I no longer had to beg and steal tampons and napkins from my three big sisters, who hogged all the good babysitting jobs. I could coast over to the side of the roller rink and buy a Coke and Pop Rocks instead of snacking on a humiliatingly down-market sandwich bag of popcorn from home. I began saving for a trip to Paris, which I thought would cost some fantastic amount like *two hundred dollars* or something. Paris was my pipedream drug of choice.

Eighth grade turned out to be a little bit okay.

On the first day of ninth grade, I was ironing my hair on the ironing board and seared a broad stripe down the front of my nose. This pretty much set the tone for my high school years: a painful, suppurating brand that advertised my social resistivity and cosmetic ineptitude. The following year, an ungainly growth spurt hit. At an unslender five-foot-twelve, my undatable fate was sealed.

My rapt audience outgrew my silly little stories. For a while I replaced the income by writing English papers for upperclassmen, but there was no joy in it, so I let that endeavor fizzle in favor of an evolving world of fiction I kept utterly secret.

It's a little unnerving to look back and see how closely all this parallels the publishing career that came my way later in life.

**WRITING A BOOK IS LIKE REARING CHILDREN—WILLPOWER HAS VERY LITTLE TO DO WITH IT.** IF YOU HAVE A LITTLE BABY CRYING IN THE MIDDLE OF THE NIGHT, AND IF YOU DEPEND ONLY ON WILLPOWER TO GET YOU OUT OF BED TO FEED THE BABY, THE BABY WILL STARVE. YOU DO IT OUT OF LOVE. WILLPOWER IS A WEAK IDEA; LOVE IS STRONG.

ANNIE DILLARD
AUTHOR OF *PILGRIM AT TINKER CREEK*

# WHAT AM I HOLDING ONTO?

Something is slowing you down. Something is energizing you. Which one are you holding onto?

Breathing in through the nose, out through the mouth:

1. Inhale on the thought: *All this I take in.*
2. Hold on the thought: *Who I am I am.*
3. Exhale on the thought: *All this I release.*
4. Hold on the thought: *Where I go I go.*

Repeat this box breathing exercise until you feel moved to write something in the space below. And then write it. Whatever it is.

WHEN A SHINING NEW IDEA EMERGES, IT OFTEN FEELS LIKE SPRINGTIME AFTER A LONG WINTER. BUT IT'S IMPORTANT TO REMEMBER THAT, THOUGH THERE IS NOTHING SO EXCITING AS RAW POTENTIAL, HARD WORK MUST ALWAYS FOLLOW. THE TRICK IS, KEEPING THAT INITIAL THRILL ALIVE THROUGHOUT THE SEASONS, LONG ENOUGH TO SET IT DOWN IN WRITING AND SHAPE IT WITH SOUND FEEDBACK AND CAREFUL EDITING. ONLY THEN CAN IT BEAR FRUIT IN THE MIND OF EVERY READER.

COLLEEN THOMPSON
AUTHOR OF *THE SALT MAIDEN*

# 3

# LET THE STORY UNFOLD ITSELF

During my surprisingly useful college career as a theatre major, part of my Stanislavsky acting training included writing character studies. Mine usually ran about forty times the recommended length, spinning out elaborate backstories and imagining offstage scenes, prompting one director to snark, "Why don't you just write a novel, for Christ sake?"

*Why didn't I?* I wonder now.

Why didn't I clap on that light bulb over my head, change my major to creative writing, and learn the proper way to write a novel instead of thrashing and reinventing wheels and feeling like a fraud for the next thirty years?

It's equally valuable to wonder why I insisted on wearing a black Danskin wrap shirt under baggy OshKosh B'Gosh overalls every day. That's just who I was at the time. It's not useful to look back and groan about it.

## NOSTALGIA OFFERS LIMP TAKEAWAY. REGRET OFFERS EVEN LESS.

I was still reading a book a day, consuming classics for the 400 level classes I was allowed to audit, side-tripping with Tom Robbins, Irving Stone, Eudora Welty, and Stephen King. I cherished books and worshipped authors. I'd written little skits and one-act plays that had been performed by various theatre troupes I'd been associated with, but it never occurred to me that I could actually write an actual book that a real publisher would really publish.

Even when I did take ownership of the idea that I wanted to write a novel, I was writing it purely for the love of laying words in a row, the same way I enjoyed latch-hooking rugs, painting, quilting, making collages from back issues of *Mother Earth News*, and a host of other creative activities one does for fun, not for a living.

I started writing that first novel, originally titled *MacPeter's Midlife Crisis*, in 1981. I dropped out of college, swore off ironing my hair, and stuffed my padded bras in the trash slot in the cramped bar car lavatory on a westbound train. I landed a sweet gig as a late-night disc jockey at a rock station in Helena, Montana.

It was a crazy time, and I fell crazy in love with a brilliant but damaged Vietnam vet twenty-some years my senior. After the war, he'd gone to college on the GI Bill, studying comp and lit, so we talked for endless whiskey-soaked hours about writing and reading, the difference between storytelling and plotting, what makes fiction true and truth bullshit, and how all good novels maintain the smell of poetry. I, meanwhile, maintained the smell of campfires, marijuana, and the carnal love of the aging English major. He introduced me to Lovecraft, Heinlein, LSD, and a gritty dose of grownup reality.

Not surprisingly, my novel was about a late-night DJ and the brilliant, damaged Vietnam vet with whom she was crazy in love. Eventually, the story required a brief epilogue featuring his untimely death, of course. I scrounged together my handwritten pages and the pieces of my broken heart, quit my disc jockey job and ran off to join the Vigilante Players, a ragged little Vaudeville-type musical theatre company.

The first time I saw my husband, he was bicycling through a blizzard. It was Groundhog Day 1983. My fellow Vigilantes and I were sitting in a window booth at the Baucus Pub in Bozeman, Montana. This great big grizzly bear of a man rode up outside, chained his bike to a parking meter, and strode off into the snow.

I said, "What kind of moron rides a bicycle in a blizzard?"

One of my friends said, "Oh, that's Gary Rodgers. You two would be great together. He's really strange, too."

Later that night, sharing backstage beers with some friends who'd just wrapped a production of *Fiddler on the Roof*, I overheard two guys grousing something on the order of, "Why can't we get some real theatre in this town instead of all this musical comedy shtick?"

As a proud professional shticktress, I felt authorized to set them straight, so I marched over and said:

## "EXCUSE ME. ANYONE WHO DOESN'T THINK COMEDY IS AN ART FORM HASN'T READ MUCH SHAKESPEARE, HAVE THEY?"

And then I launched into a lengthy diatribe about everything from Molière and the French neo-classics to Jerry Lewis in *The Nutty Professor*. When I paused to inhale, Gary stepped forward, enveloped me in his arms, and said, "I love you."

Three hours later, I said it back.

An intellectual fisherman ten years older than me, Gary lived in a tiny, woodstove-heated cabin on the downhill end of a buffalo ranch in the Bridger Mountains. In addition to his original college degree, his continuing education addiction included a heaping mishmash of credits that added up to minors or BAs in History and Political Science, an associate degree in Culinary Art, and later, a degree in Airframe and Powerplant Mechanics. He used to joke that becoming a lawyer would have been hard on his conscience, so he'd used his original degree in Criminal Justice to become a criminal.

This didn't play well with my conservative Christian parents, who were horrified when they learned we were living in sin. They were not at all comforted when I called on a Thursday night to tell them we were getting married Saturday morning. The only clergy we could get on such short notice was a tiny Indian woman who preached every Sunday morning from the roof of the local A&W Root Beer stand. We dragged my sister and her family, a few friends, and several dogs up into the mountains for an impromptu post-hippie, pseudo-Native American nuptial encounter, only to discover it was the opening day of grouse hunting season. So it turned out to be an actual shotgun wedding with baying hounds instead of an organist and the continuous crack of rifle fire instead of church bells.

Please, don't be distracted by some Woodiwissian notion of love at first sight or fate or anything heartsy-flowery. Predictably—inevitably—this marriage was a disaster. I was way too young, still trying to figure out who I was in the world. Gary was appalled to discover that I'd never learned to drive and could hardly ride a bicycle. I discovered that he read Edward Albee and A. B. Guthrie, which bored me silly, and he kept wanting to go winter camping, which is just effing wrong. Our shooting star of a love affair rapidly cooled to an earthbound lump of mineral deposits in a crater of dirty dishes and mutual disappointment.

I did try. On our anniversary, I gave the Griz a pair of lovebirds as a symbol of our holy bond.

"You and the parables," he groaned. It was one of the many things that made him want to bang his head against a wall.

In the following weeks, Mr. Lovebird wouldn't let Mrs. Lovebird near the food and water, so she starved to death. But she used her last ounce of strength to peck a mortal wound in his head.

## THE POWER OF PARABLE IS UNDENIABLE.

My suggestion was a no-fault divorce. Gary's idea was to answer an ad looking for two-person teams to staff fire lookout towers in Northern California.

"If we go out there and live on top of a mountain in a fourteen-by-fourteen-foot box for nine months," he said, "when we come down, we'll either be happily married or happily divorced."

True that. Plus, it just seemed like an extraordinary thing to do, and I never aspired to be ordinary, so—yeah! I was excited. We sold everything we owned, which didn't take long, and off we went to Weaver Bally, a blunt, balding peak in the Shasta-Trinity National Forest. We had a stunning view of the Trinity Alps from our outhouse. Our Forest Service radio was powered by a solar battery. Everything else was powered by us. We had a few propane lamps, cooked on a hibachi out on the catwalk, bathed in an ice-cold creek, and carried water from a spring about half a mile down the mountain.

The first day, I went down to the spring with two five-gallon jugs, feeling like Nature Woman. Stands Without Blow Dryer. I filled the jugs, started back up the mountain, and ... sheesh. They were really heavy. *Ugh!* I groaned inwardly.

## DOING EXTRAORDINARY STUFF IS HARD!

Apply this seemingly simple truth as needed to publishing and life. Repeat three times, and then get over it. You're welcome.

I stopped and poured a little water out of each jug. Went another forty yards or so. Poured out a little more water. Went a little farther. Poured out a little more. By the time I got back to the fire tower, I had about two tablespoons of water left, my nose was gushing blood from the altitude, and I seriously wanted that divorce.

The pile of paper in my novel box swelled with angrily scribbled scenes about sex and death and the Gordian knot of a doomed love affair.

As we labored through the spring, I wondered if the other lookout teams were taking advantage of the bucolic seclusion to have non-stop nasty nature sex. Nothing like that was happening on Weaver Bally.

Gary and I slept in separate sleeping bags on a plywood shelf next to the Osborne Fire Finder. We fought when we could no longer ignore each other, hauled water, and took turns manning the binoculars and radio. We spent hundreds of hours playing Scrabble, reading, and staring into space.

Once a month, we went down to Weaverville for supplies and were able to swap out our big box of reading materials at a rickety store that sold used books, old magazines, shabby household items, and rusty small engine junk. On one particularly fruitful excursion, I scored a stack of *Rolling Stone* back issues and a nice selection of trade paperbacks, including T.C. Boyle's *The Women* and the Dinesen/Blixen soul-wrencher *Out of Africa*. Gary laid hands on the James Clavell *Shogun* series, a slug of mass paperback thrillers, and several hefty physics and trigonometry textbooks, which he described as "just for fun."

"That's your idea of fun?" I said.

He glared at me as if I'd spat on Gandhi. "What the hell's not fun about physics?" How, how, how was this divorce not inevitable? I'm still baffled.

Gary also insisted on buying a large, round balsa wood cheese box, and I objected to the expenditure. We were struggling to get by on the minimal wage ("minimum wage" would be overstating) we were being paid to supply the Forest Service with two warm bodies in a box.

"Gary, there's no money for extras," I said. "Why do we need that?"

"Say, for example, some people were coming over," he said, patiently, "and we wanted to, say, tie some knots. You'd keep your knot-tying supplies in this."

I stared at him for a long moment and then blurted, "*Who the fuck are you?*" before I took my non-algebra books to the cash register.

You may be asking me the same question right now or at least wondering what any of this has to do with writing.

Well … nothing. And everything.

Nothing because it's not about pen-on-paper writing. Everything because stories only happen in the context of life. The most important thing we do to feed the many-tentacled writer octobeast is *live*.

## LIVE. LOVE. LISTEN. GET BUSY. GET ANGRY. GET OVER IT. THEN WRITE ABOUT IT.

Nora Ephron said in an NPR interview: "My religion is 'Get over it.' And I was raised in that religion … my mother saying, 'Everything is copy. Everything is material. Someday you will think this is funny.' … It was work through it, get to the other side, turn it into something." That mindset worked for her, and, for the most part, it has worked for me.

Throughout our nine months on the fire tower, I kept a journal, but about three months in, having tired of chronicling the litany of Gary's absurd foibles and offenses, I began dabbling at my novel in earnest, filling several yellow legal pads with character notes, scene work, and an elaborate plan for the arc of the story. When my notebook supply ran out, I used a pattern-making workbook that had lots of white space in and around the diagrams and step-by-step instructions for plain peasant blouses and tiered hippie skirts.

I found myself trying to fit dialogue and descriptions into the available openings. There was no reason for the words to fit into this pattern book; I figured I'd copy it into a proper notebook someday—maybe even type it up if I ever got a typewriter—but I enjoyed the wordplay, the weighing of prose and dialogue, the conscious questioning:

## IS THIS WORD TRULY EARNING THE SPACE IT'S TAKING UP?

Is this sentence, this syllable, truly needed? Does this paragraph fit, or is it just a superfluous cheese box of knot-tying supplies?

I didn't realize the practical value of this exercise until years later when I started writing my weekly syndicated newspaper column, "Earth to Joni."

HarperCollins had sent me out on one of those big book tours publishers used to orchestrate. My editor, Marjorie Braman, was concerned that I wasn't writing consistently while I traveled, so she wisely suggested I hook up an Erma Bombeck-type seven-hundred-word-per-week personal essay column, featuring wry observations about politics, pop culture, and my hippie take on motherhood.

The column gig obligated me to crank out something of substance on a weekly deadline. The anecdote-based format, which I described as "three *ha!*s and a *hmm*," schooled me in the elegance of structure. The slender word count reminded me that brevity is the soul of wit. It worked the same writing muscles I'd started building with the pattern book exercises years earlier. I learned to weigh my prose in a way I wouldn't have, had I stuck with the limitless college-ruled filler paper form of novel writing.

Writing a novel is like cultivating an English garden; you have all the room you need to create lily ponds and pathways and labyrinths. An essay is a careful arrangement of cut flowers in a vase; you collect one essential aspect of a story and clear away everything that distracts from it.

The takeaway here is the value of experimenting with a different format. Break away from a chapter that's got you mired and take twenty minutes to write a poem, prayer, or grocery list. Get off the computer and write longhand for an afternoon. Play around with haiku or the 140-character limitations of Twitter—if you can resist falling down the Twitter rabbit hole of BS.

Recently, when I was feeling stuck, I took a raft of manuscript pages from my recycling bin, turned them upside down and rewrote the same scene longhand between the printed lines. Fitting the narrative around the serpentine ass-over-teakettle dialogue, I thought about that old pattern book. Weighing each word, I was forced to make decisions about the essence of the scene, to make sure every syllable worked in service of the story.

Toward the end of the 1984 fire season, a number of serious blazes broke out, and Griz was the star eagle eye of the forest, calling a number of incidents on the thinnest wisps of smoke, locating them with uncanny precision, which impressed the Redding Hot Shots, who were pretty full of themselves and not easily impressed. He stood out on the catwalk, scanning the Alps and valleys by day. By night, he'd set up his big reflecting telescope and explore the stars, cross-referencing constellations and asteroids in his dog-eared library of chunky astronomy guidebooks. I was getting pretty good with words, but I didn't know how to tell him how beautiful he was, this earthbound man engrossed in the sky.

Miles from any hint of unnatural light, the darkness on the mountain was a dimension unto itself. This was the kind of darkness that takes you beyond your own little galaxy. Everything you always believed to be huge is revealed as utterly insignificant.

Gary tried to show me the Orion nebula, and I got frustrated, straining in the eyepiece.

"Babe," he said, "you have to use averted vision."

"What does that mean?"

## "STOP TRYING SO HARD, AND IT'LL ALL SWIM INTO VIEW."

Sound advice for astronomy, life, and writing.

Night after night, I looked up at those stars with a growing certainty that my role in this vast, magical universe was simply to be, and nothing about my being was predetermined or burdened with expectation unless I allowed others to make it that. I knew that I was a writer, but I was a writer for myself first. The idea of anyone reading or judging my words was somewhere off in the cosmos of my averted vision. I was free to breathe and re-breathe my words however I wanted without fear. This is a gift I would not have had if my sensible side had nudged me to become an English major in college. I would have been trained to criticize myself and others without ever knowing the true, star-spangled freedom of writing for myself. For the joy of setting words in rows.

By late autumn, Weaver Bally was blanketed with snow, and the tower was swaddled in fog and cloud cover for hours, sometimes days at a time. You couldn't see your hand in front of your face, so we dared not step out on the icy rocks. Gary tied a rope line we could follow from the bottom of the tower to the door of the outhouse at the edge of the cliff. As we huddled inside by the propane heater, I made it winter in my novel. Making use of the hard knot of cold fixed at my midsection, I sussed out the first version of an ending that made the story feel sort of complete, if not actually finished.

One day during our morning chores, Gary unzipped our separate sleeping bags, laid his open on the plywood, spread mine over it, and zipped the two together.

"To conserve body heat," he said gruffly. "We'll stay warmer."

Carl Sagan:

## "FOR SMALL CREATURES SUCH AS WE, THE VASTNESS IS BEARABLE ONLY THROUGH LOVE."

I tucked our pillows in next to each other, resigning myself to the fact that I was stupid in love with this stranger I'd married, and, inexplicably, he was stupid in love with me. We both recognized that our entanglement could never be undone without tremendous mutual damage to our deepest root systems. Resolving to keep the proverbial law of kindness in our mouths, we replaced our traditional ideas about marriage with a monogamous, mutually respecting "you do you" pact that, at this writing, has held up astonishingly well for about forty years.

Gary and I have very little in common. He's ten years older than me. We frequently disagree on politics, religion, finances, and the disposition of our children, but we've learned to disagree lovingly. Things get mean only often enough to remind us that we must and will be more careful in the future. I guess I would qualify our relationship as "comfortably incompatible." He is, without exception, the most interesting person I've ever met, and I enjoy being able to say that about my spouse. We travel well together and do the *New York Times* crossword puzzle every day without fail—two dynamics that are key to both our longevity as a couple and my success as a writer.

Early on, Gary made the conscious decision not to read my books.

"Because I don't want you to feel like I'm looking over your shoulder while you're doing your work," he told me, which is a gift, but I worry sometimes about what the blowback will be when that work makes its way out into the world. My novels make it pretty clear that I'm bisexual, and my memoir included some intensely personal information about our relationship. I've offered Gary opportunities to voice an objection before information about our private life was published, but he's always stood by his pledge and preserved that critique-free space where I am loved and respected without reservation. This is so courageous and so—I'm gonna say it—*manly* of him, it brings tears to my eyes.

Muriel Rukeyser:

> ## "WHAT WOULD HAPPEN IF ONE WOMAN TOLD THE TRUTH ABOUT HER LIFE? THE WORLD WOULD SPLIT OPEN."

A destructive (and not infrequent) element that effects my ghostwriting projects is well-meaning input from spouses and other significant others. It doesn't matter if the spouse is a Pulitzer-winning novelist or a tax attorney who doesn't know shit from shingles about writing; they feel it's their duty to read a rough draft, compare it to the latest bestsellers and rip it to shreds. So here's my client sitting on this delicate robin's egg of a story, and here's me, gently tending them, lending the structure of a creative nest. Along comes the client's brilliant college-age daughter or dickhead husband, cracks that precious egg on a griddle, and tells us, "Oh, this'll never fly. You didn't even put feathers on it. Let me tell you how to glue feathers on it. That will fix it." I try to reassure my clients that this springs from a loving intent, but the damage is done. There's no scraping the creative process back into its protective shell. The effect is disruptive at best and, at worst, ruinous.

Every time I see it happen, I fly home and hug the stuffing out of my Gare Bear. Every time our daughter Jerusha breaks up with a less than supportive boyfriend, she says, "Daddy has set the bar impossibly high."

Being the spouse of an author can be a financial, emotional, and logistical nightmare at times. For the most part, Gary bicycles through these blizzards without complaint, and for that, he's been rewarded with a partner who is (for the most part) happy and financially successful.

I would be a writer with or without him. But being a writer with him is a lot more fun.

IF YOU GAVE ME A CHOICE, ALFIE, BETWEEN LOVE AND TRUST, I'D CHOOSE TRUST EVERY TIME. LOVE YOU CAN GET IN THE BARGAIN BASEMENT ON SPECIAL OFFER. TRUST IS MUCH MORE EXPENSIVE. AND HARDER TO FIND.

LINDA GILLARD
FROM *HOUSE OF SILENCE*

# WHAT AM I NOT SEEING?

A useful exercise I call "Character Divination" uses an ancient Tarot spread to ask questions that develop characters and firm up the foundation of a story. I have a few super cool oracle decks that feature fabulous art, but I don't use typical Tarot cards. In Plot Whispering sessions, I've done it on a white board with blank sticky notes. There's no meaning attached to the card itself; the art is meant to provoke thought beyond the obvious. You're not on a quest to draw mystic answers from the universe; you're relaxing into your peripheral vision, allowing yourself to see the answers already waiting there.

The spread looks like this:

```
        3               10
                         9
  6  1X2  5              8
                         7
        4
```

Card 1 = Who is this character?

Card 2 (crossing Card 1) = What obstacles/influences oppose the character?

Card 3 = What is the character consciously thinking?

Card 4 = What is the character subconsciously feeling?

Card 5 = What is the character's motivating desire?

Card 6 = What are the inescapable influences from the character's past?

Card 7 = Who are the people surrounding the character?

Card 8 = What is the environment surrounding the character?

Card 9 = What must the character learn in order to evolve?

Card 10 = What is the character's ultimate destiny in this story?

LIFE SHRINKS OR EXPANDS
ACCORDING TO ONE'S
COURAGE.

ANAÏS NIN
AUTHOR OF *DELTA OF VENUS*

# 4

# FIRST ONE'S FREE

**W**hen people ask me about my first book, I cite my first novel *Crazy for Trying*—my first published book—the first one that counts, in my mind, not because it's the first one that succeeded by the usual metrics, but because it's the first one I genuinely cared about.

My *first* book was a bit of a misfire.

In the years after Gary and I rejoined civilization, I worked as a disc jockey and voiceover artist. I wrote advertising copy, Christmas letters, and radio plays. I composed songs and comedy skits for my theatre friends and children's plays for my theatre school students. Our son Malachi was born in 1987, Jerusha in 1989. We moved to the Philly area so Gary could take a job as an airline mechanic, and I was, for the most part, a stay-at-home mom, filling in with temp office work as needed.

On Mother's Day 1991, he gave me my first computer with a card that said, "This is to show I know your brain hasn't turned to Wheatena."

"You always said you wanted to write," he shrugged. "You should give it a try."

James M. Cain:

> **"THIS BUNKUM AND STINKUM OF COLLEGE CREATIVE WRITING COURSES! THE ONLY THING YOU CAN DO FOR SOMEONE WHO WANTS TO WRITE IS TO BUY HIM A TYPEWRITER."**

After some swearing and struggling as I learned my way around the computer, I briskly cranked out a manuscript entitled *Kids in the Sky: A Complete Guide to Safe, Happy Air Travel with Little Tykes*. Because "write what you know," right? This was a topic about which I knew a great deal, because Gary's job with the airline had blessed us with flight benefits; we could fly anywhere for free. We had to fly standby, so we couldn't really plan—we had to fly by the seat of our pants and be prepared to swivel at any moment—but that was part of the adventure. Our kids had logged well over two hundred thousand air miles by the time they started preschool.

Seeing how less experienced children and parents struggled, I was positive my book was extremely marketable. In my mind, that was a good reason to write a book. I went to the bookstore, looked at the travel books, jotted down the names and addresses of the publishers and typed up a round of stiffly businesslike "Dear Sir/Ma'am" query letters, offering the nameless but amazingly lucky editors the opportunity to publish my brilliantly funny and helpful book.

You will be shocked to hear that every editor and agent I queried either responded with a form rejection or ignored me completely.

*What the hell?* Did these fools not recognize an instant bestseller when they saw one? Did these bastards not care about the safety of children? Did these troglodytes not appreciate the 120 flight attendant surveys I'd collected or the time I'd invested in removing the side-strips from the dot matrix printer paper? What kind of jaded New York piss-widget could resist all those adorable anecdotes about my precocious children?

Gary encouraged me not to give up after all the hard work I'd done, but I said, "What else can I do? I've queried *everyone*."

In fact, I'd sent out maybe a dozen queries, but that felt like a lot, and the dozen slap-in-the-face rejections made it feel like a lot more. Screw that. I shoved the manuscript in a box that ended up ... somewhere. Who cares? I didn't. I'd written this book for one reason: I thought I could sell it.

Years later, Laurie Harper, my first literary agent offered me a wise bit of advice that I pass on to every would-be memoirist I meet:

## "YOU HAVE TO GET WHAT YOU NEED FROM THE WRITING OF A BOOK, BECAUSE THE REST IS A CRAPSHOOT."

The fact is, I put very little soul into that book and got very little joy out of it. And it showed. A book written for money carries the unmistakable stench of cash-hankering, and very few can rise above it, because—trust me—someone else out there is prepared to put heart and soul into a book on that topic.

Back in the 1980s, I took Gary's fire tower copy of *The Big Sky* to be signed by A. B. Guthrie at a bookstore in Helena, Montana. I was the only reader who showed up for this Pulitzer-winning novelist's book signing. (A source of great comfort to me during disappointing bookstore events of my own down the road.) He sat in a rocking chair, and I sat on the floor next to him, chatting amiably for over an hour.

During the course of that conversation, he said:

## "WHATEVER YOU NEED TO SAY, IT SHOULD BE AT LEAST AS VALUABLE AS THE PAPER."

It's too easy to forget that, now that we're typing on computers instead of killing trees, but it's the time that matters anyway.

And if you can stand to take the parable of the pattern book a step further, I'll add this: You don't stop writing because you run out of notebooks. Whatever you think you're lacking—a better computer, a nice home office, six weeks at a writer's retreat—you don't need any of that to do your work. You most certainly don't need a book deal. In fact, a book deal is literally and figuratively the last thing you need. An agent's approval and a green light from an acquisitions editor are great, but they don't endow you with the right or the reason to write a book.

The imperative to write lies within you. A book deal simply offers one option for where to put the book when you're done.

I continued to noodle at my novel off and on. I enjoyed revisiting it, but as a voracious and astute reader, I compared it to Fannie Flagg, Stephen King, Carrie Fisher, and Gore Vidal, and compared to their books, mine was a God-awful piece of crap.

My friend Susan wanted to read it, though, so I let her, and she genuinely loved it. She happened to be dating an English professor, so she made him read it, too, and over dinner, he told me he was actually very impressed. He delivered enough candid criticism to validate the praise and enough candid praise that the criticism wasn't crippling. He offered some pointed edits.

"Only one 'keening' per novel."

"Watch out for the secondary story arc; it needs at least a modicum of foreshadowing in the first forty pages."

More important, he talked about it as if it were a novel, not a "novel." A project, not a plaything.

"You have talent," he said, "but it comes off as untrained. You should enroll in some creative writing courses. Maybe think about getting a degree."

Gary and I discussed the possibility of me going back to school when Jerusha started kindergarten the following autumn, but I honestly never felt like my lack of a college degree was standing between me and writing. My parents are both accomplished professional musicians, and neither of them had any formal training. They hammered it out on talent and hard work. I figured I should be able to do the same.

It resonated for me when I read Joan Didion's assertion in *Slouching Toward Bethlehem*:

> **"GRAMMAR IS A PIANO I PLAY BY EAR. ALL I KNOW ABOUT GRAMMAR IS ITS POWER."**

I went back to Strunk and White and refreshed my respect for the rules that must be fully understood to be beautifully broken. I did some revisions, implementing the professor's suggestions, astonished to find that, dang, this thing really did not suck. I allowed myself to imagine that maybe I could get it published.

My sister Janis had been working on a romance novel and hooked up with her local RWA (Romance Writers of America) chapter, and from what I absorbed, these women were shaking the publishing tree big time. These were businesswomen, not dabblers. They had a passion for their craft and had honed the query process down to laser surgery.

Janis sent me Jeff Herman's guide to literary agents and a *Publishers Marketplace* that was only a year old. After some study on the proper way to go about it, I sent out a round of carefully crafted queries and collected a round of slaps in the face. But it didn't sting as much this time. And the next round of rejections stung a little less.

Many of the rejection letters offered encouraging words about my writing in general and listed specific suggestions for improving the book. Several of them confirmed the professor's diagnosis: I had talent, but needed training, and they didn't have the time or desire to tutor me, particularly with a manuscript that had bloated beyond six hundred pages. All of them gave the least creative but most important advice: Keep writing.

Margaret Atwood:

## "A WORD AFTER A WORD AFTER A WORD IS POWER."

In 1994, Jerusha turned five, and I started making plans for my return to college, thinking that once I knew how to do it properly, I'd revamp this novel and maybe write another. Realistically, I figured, a degree would more likely be the on-ramp to a real job as an English teacher or librarian, which would mesh well with motherhood while feeding my reading and writing addictions.

Gary was transferred to Houston, Texas, that summer. I celebrated Jerusha's first day of school, knowing that the following semester, I'd be taking my first step toward becoming a real writer. Meanwhile, I signed with a terrific talent agent and was doing radio commercial voiceovers.

One morning, as I was getting ready to go to the recording studio, I was braiding my long auburn hair, and Gary leaned down to kiss me on the neck.

With his lips close to my jaw, he said, "What the hell is that?"

I teased him about being an inept sweet-talker. But Gary told me later, "That was the moment I knew you had cancer."

*FIND OUT THE REASON THAT COMMANDS YOU TO WRITE;* SEE WHETHER IT HAS SPREAD ITS ROOTS INTO THE VERY DEPTH OF YOUR HEART; CONFESS TO YOURSELF YOU WOULD HAVE TO DIE IF YOU WERE FORBIDDEN TO WRITE.

RAINER MARIA RILKE
AUTHOR OF *LETTERS TO A YOUNG POET*

# WHAT'S MY MOTIVATION?

According to playwright David Mamet, motivation is key to action. Every scene in any book or play should answer three questions:

- Who wants what from whom?
- What happens if they don't get it?
- Why now?

Thinking about any given scene in your own story—the writer in search of self—or the story you're trying to tell in your current writing project. Are Mamet's questions answered?

*WRITE WHAT YOU FEEL AND WHAT YOU KNOW. **WRITE WHAT DRIVES YOUR HEART, NOT WHAT DRIVES THE MARKET.** IT TAKES COURAGE AND PERSISTENCE TO FIND YOUR VOICE. YOU MIGHT HAVE TO WRITE A MILLION WORDS, BUT ULTIMATELY, IN DOING SO, YOU WILL FORGE YOUR OWN UNIQUE PATH. AND THEN, AS YOU PASS THROUGH WHAT CAN BE LONG MONTHS OF DOUBT AND SOUL-KILLING REJECTION, YOU WILL BE ARMORED IN YOUR OWN TRUTH. THAT IN ITSELF WILL SUSTAIN YOU AND BRING YOU SATISFACTION AND JOY.*

BARBARA TAYLOR SISSEL
AUTHOR OF *EVIDENCE OF LIFE*

# 5

# DON'T FEAR THE REAPER

I didn't write a memoir about cancer because I had cancer; I wrote it because I'm a writer. Cancer is not the story of my life. It's not even the most interesting thing that's ever happened to me. I tell everyone who asks my advice about writing a cancer-themed memoir that the least interesting aspect of the story is the *effing cancer*. The problem is, cancer kicks down the door and sits on your lap like a nine-thousand-pound gorilla, looming so large, it's hard to see anything else. In that moment, it's imperative that you remember: like stories, cancer exists only in the context of a life. That life is what you fight for. The moment you lose your focus on life, you have forfeited the light to the darkness.

## THE MOST IMPORTANT THING TO KEEP IN MIND AS YOU WRITE YOUR MEMOIR: IT'S NOT ABOUT YOU.

A good memoir is rooted in common ground you share with the reader, and the best memoirs are rooted in common ground we all share as human beings. Events offer a skeleton for a memoir, but the blood and guts reside in relationships, themes, and character arcs.

If the cancer schtick is of interest to you, there's more about that experience in *Bald in the Land of Big Hair*.

(Spoiler alert: I lived!)

For our purposes here, long story short, after a series of doctors insisted there was nothing wrong with me, Gary bulldozed through the HMO to a specialist who knew immediately what he was looking at. For months, my insurance refused to authorize a biopsy (a Christian Scientist HMO, apparently), but eventually, I was diagnosed with non-Hodgkin's lymphoma: a virulent blood cancer. Tumors had manifested in lymph nodes below my right jaw and metastasized to both sides of my neck and chest, but the cancer itself is systemic, so the standard treatment at the time was aggressive chemotherapy followed by radiation and bone marrow transplant.

The first day, Dr. Ro, my wonderful little Korean oncologist, told me that I had "less than 50 percent chance of long-term survival." She later clarified that this actually meant 15–20 percent, and "long-term" meant five years. Beyond that, my odds of survival were "statistically negligible."

The first day, a nurse gave me a stack of brochures:

*Facts About Lymphoma*

*Coping With End of Life Issues*

*Chemotherapy and You*

My immediate reaction was "No. Effing. Way."

Not me. *Chemotherapy and the Guy Who Invented Pantyhose*, maybe. Not chemotherapy and me. I intended to investigate my alternatives.

"Your alternatives," Ro said, "are chemotherapy and death."

"I'll do herbal medicine," I protested. "I'll meditate and pray. I'll become a vegetarian!"

"How will you do all that if you're dead?" she asked calmly.

"That's the only way I'd ever become a vegetarian," said Gary.

It was a relief to laugh. There would be a lot of moments like that in the coming months. One of us would make some little wisecrack, like a cartoon character opening a spindly umbrella as an anvil plummets toward his head.

Though it often goes undiagnosed in the whirling maelstrom of side effects, devastations, and self-shitting terror that accompany this disease, post-traumatic stress disorder is not uncommon in cancer patients. The body and mind are subjected to fifty shades of physical and emotional contaminant. People around you are dying, losing limbs, losing hope, letting go. You look in the mirror and see Uncle Fester. You look at your lover and see unmitigated grief.

More than once, Gary clamped my face between his big hands and forced my eyes to meet his and said, "*Stop it.* You can't panic. You can't look to the right or left. You look *here.* Straight ahead."

Loving someone with cancer is exhausting, which makes loving someone who loves you when you have cancer a guilty, drain-circling drag.

I was on a regimen called CHOP+Bleo, a cocktail featuring Adriamycin, which causes a variety of infamous side effects. Ro told me I would lose my hair, so I was mentally prepared to be bald. I was not prepared to be a browless, pubeless gecko with no eyelashes. As my white blood cells were systematically eradicated, I hardly went out of the house for fear a random germ might cross the path of my stumbling drunk of an immune system, like a serial killer at a bachelorette party.

Gary worked the night shift in a massive hangar at George Bush Intercontinental Airport. On a typical chemo day, he got off work at 7:30 a.m., helped me get the kids off to school, drove me downtown to Dr. Ro's office, sat taking notes and asking questions during the appointment, took me to the lab for bloodwork and then to the chemo infusion place if my white count could tolerate another five-hour IV onslaught while he went around running errands and getting my prescriptions, then drove home through the rush hour traffic, poured me into bed, cleaned out whatever receptacle I'd used for vomiting in the car, collected the kids, helped with homework, fed them dinner, put them to bed, and went back to work all night again.

Ironically, people kept telling him how brave I was. They, of course, saw my brave sick person face, the spackled-on positive attitude. Only Gary witnessed the enormous anger and depression, which escalated when I was hit with premature menopause. (Insert "mad cow disease" joke here.)

On one particularly bad day, I told him, "Gare Bear, I wouldn't blame you if you had to escape from all this."

He touched my cheek and said, "Where would I escape to? You're my whole life. And sometimes … life is a bitch."

To say I'm grateful to this man is almost as inadequate as saying I love him; even now, after decades as a seasoned word-slinger, I have not the poetry nor prose to express what he means to me.

Cancer is isolating in the best circumstances, but having just moved to Houston a few months before I was diagnosed, I knew almost no one in this town, and I wasn't in great shape to strike up new acquaintances.

"Hi, I'm Joni. I'm a sucking black hole of emotional need right now. My hobbies are drugs and napping, and I often need emergency childcare in the middle of the night. Wanna be my friend?"

I didn't get out much, and everywhere I did go was just one more place I didn't belong. My own closet was an unfamiliar warehouse of medical supplies, syringes, and biohazardous waste receptacles. My daily routine fragmented into a jerky agenda of appointments, IVs, and procedures. Most of my friends expressed a sympathetic gasp and exited stage left, replaced by a costumed cast of technicians and clinicians. The ongoing dialogue was a sterile Esperanto: anagrams, medical terms, and the careful, lilting rhetoric of disappointing test results.

The only place I had any peace of mind—any illusion of being in control, any strength of wit, any sense of belonging—was the home I'd created in my novel. In that world, I knew every side street and stick of furniture. I'd personally laid hands on each tree trunk and bathtub.

## A GOOD NOVEL IS ENGINEERED TO ACCOMMODATE HARD LOVE.

The characters were as scarred and foolish as my scarred, foolish heart. I lay in bed with them, listening to the layers of conversation, the spoken and unspoken exchanges. I nudged them toward each other, and I loved it when the story nudged back.

One day, mapping my remaining chemo cycles on a calendar in the back of a new pocketbook, I discovered a little cardstock foldout that displayed a neat grid of the next five years: January 1, 1995, to January 1, 2000. All the air went out of me when I realized I was very likely looking at the rest of my life.

Jerusha was almost six now; Malachi was seven-and-a-half. Soon they would remember very little of the person I was before cancer. If I died before they turned ten, they'd remember very little of me at all. If I was lucky, I would see Malachi turn twelve. I hoped Gary would find a woman of good quality so he wouldn't have to handle two teenagers by himself.

I dredged up that *Coping With End of Life Issues* workbook and spent several hours noodling through it, surprised to find that this pragmatic nod to the probability of my death actually freed up some mental real estate for the possibilities of my life. Given this concise foldaway card of years, I would have to be specific about what I needed and unsparingly honest about what I could expect. It should be intention oriented, I decided, not driven by circumstances, because circumstances were predictably FUBAR.

There was no way I could invest four years in college now. I'd had the opportunity to get an education: a full ride scholarship when I was a teenager. I screwed that away, partying and doing plays. There was no getting it back. The important thing now was to live my life in a way that felt full, so I could leave in peace at any given moment, no bitterness, no unfinished business, no sense of not enough. That has nothing to do with a number of years, I already knew. As a tweenage candy-striper at an old folks home, I'd seen people die in their nineties feeling cheated.

## ENOUGH IS A QUALITY, NOT A QUANTITY.

My Five Year Plan was, of necessity, pretty simple. The priority was to lay a foundation from which my family could go forward. I narrowed this to two clear objectives:

One: a handprint of lovingkindness. I would focus on leaving a single indelible impression on my children every day, hoping it would form a specific thread for them to pull when they were ready someday to unravel their memories of me.

Two: one good book. I would focus all my creative energy on that single selfish goal that would allow me to die without feeling like a loser.

This was my rope in the fog. I know well-meaning people would spin-doctor me into a much nicer person after I was dead; I wanted to make sure the grownup Malachi and Jerusha would be able to find me. I wanted them to be able to say, "My mother was a writer."

Iris Murdoch:

> **"WRITING IS LIKE GETTING MARRIED. ONE SHOULD NEVER COMMIT ONESELF UNTIL ONE IS AMAZED AT ONE'S LUCK."**

I was amazed. I was humbly, hugely, gratefully amazed.

Not very convenient, I must say, to discover your purpose in life simultaneously to accepting that you are about to die, but the realization was still a thrill, and I can't think of a more effective catalyst for applying oneself.

It seemed important to establish a workspace for myself.

Mom's Office. No Barbies or Legos allowed.

We lived in a small apartment, so this wasn't going to be an actual room of one's own. More of a concept, really. But a concept with tangible borders. I got Gary to pull the sofa about two feet out from the wall, and behind it, I stacked three banana boxes I'd begged from the produce department at Fiesta. Gary topped it with a section of Formica countertop rescued from a dumpster and set my computer on it. Whatever life took place in the living room, it didn't cross the back of the sofa while Mom was working in Mom's Office.

I read and reread John Gardner's *The Art of Fiction: Notes on Craft for Young Writers*, boxing technical and artistic takeaway with color coded highlighters:

> **"FICTION DOES NOT SPRING INTO THE WORLD FULLY GROWN, LIKE ATHENA. IT IS THE PROCESS OF WRITING AND REWRITING THAT MAKES A FICTION ORIGINAL, IF NOT PROFOUND."**

I made another brutal pass through my novel, now titled *Last Chance Gulch*, check-listing all the criticisms and suggestions I'd gotten from the rejecting editors and agents and a few trusted friends who functioned as beta readers. I incorporated the changes that resonated with me and left the rest for critics to incorporate in their own novels if they so chose.

After pruning a lot (though not nearly enough) of the elegant variation, gratuitous guitar-playing and extraneous chit-chat, I invested in an updated *Publisher's Marketplace* and a box of continuous feed paper for my dot matrix printer and started a query rotation. Twenty packages went out: query letter, SASE, and twenty-five pages of manuscript. Every time I got a rejection, I put another query in the pipeline, usually within the hour.

I also started writing another novel. Not because I felt compelled to crank something out as Plan B, but because I'd come to understand something about myself: writing made me happy. I needed that world to retreat to, those beds to roll around in, those confrontations and confessions on which to eavesdrop. It didn't just give me pleasure; it gave me purpose. I was sick enough now that there wasn't much else I could physically do in a day, and people really didn't expect anything of me, but on the off chance anyone asked, I could honestly say, "I'm writing a book."

The response to that was usually a wan, patronizing smile. No one expected me to get this pig published. Of course, they didn't say so, because when you have cancer, people try very hard to say the right thing, the upbeat thing, the supportive "I'll pray for you" thing that (in theory) is supposed to make you feel better, but usually just makes them feel better about themselves. Bless their hearts. In retrospect, "I'll pray for you" is probably an appropriate thing to say to anyone writing a book, whether they have cancer or not.

We soldiered on toward summer. By the end of chemo, Gary and I had been forced into bankruptcy, and I was utterly depleted physically and emotionally. Things got very dark for a while, but it was the kind of dark that takes you beyond your own little galaxy. It's not as bad now as it used to be, but back then, if an aggressive course of chemo left you alive, it didn't leave you much else. I tried to tell myself that was enough. For the moment, I was in remission, alive and writing.

Henry David Thoreau:

> ## "HOW VAIN IT IS TO SIT DOWN TO WRITE WHEN YOU HAVE NOT STOOD UP TO LIVE."

I get paid to joke about it now, but it wasn't funny at the time. It was so not funny that even now, all these years later, I occasionally wake up in the middle of the night with my heart hammering. I don't want to dwell on my cancer experience, sucking on it like a lifelong jawbreaker until my tongue gets bloody, but I can't deny the extent to which it rewrote the landscape of my life and continues to color my perceptions and choices as a woman and a writer—not necessarily in a bad way, but in a way that I know is frustrating to people who don't understand, and I do feel bad about that sometimes.

For me, in the crucible moment of chemo, the integrity and survival of that first novel was truly a matter of life and death. I was convinced that if this book didn't exist, my children would never truly know me. Now I know no other life but writing. I have no fallback position for making a living: a luxury that occasionally sucks but keeps me mindful.

**THE MOST IMPORTANT THINGS ARE THE HARDEST TO SAY. THEY ARE THE THINGS YOU GET ASHAMED OF, BECAUSE WORDS DIMINISH THEM.**

STEPHEN KING
AUTHOR OF *ON WRITING*

## WHAT ELSE?

Use this space to create something other than written words. Color, glue, shred, fold—whatever you feel like doing—and while you do it, ponder the percentage of your life that is dedicated to the creation of words.

What does it mean to you?

What does it mean to the reader?

**ALWAYS READ YOUR DIALOGUE ALOUD.** IF IT MAKES YOU CRINGE (WHICH HAPPENS TO ME OFTEN ON THE FIRST ROUND), IF IT COMES OUT SOUNDING LIKE WORDS NO ONE EVER SPOKE, YOU HAVE YOUR WORK CUT OUT FOR YOU. TAKE TIME TO LISTEN TO THE WAY PEOPLE TALK. CONVERSATIONS RARELY FOLLOW A PERFECTLY LOGICAL ARC, AND UNLESS YOUR CHARACTER IS A SEASONED TELEVISION PERSONALITY, HE OR SHE WILL NOT UTTER ELEGANT PARAGRAPHS. NEVER USE DIALOGUE TO DELIVER BACKSTORY ("REMEMBER WHEN WE GOT DIVORCED TEN YEARS AGO?"). FINALLY, PEOPLE RARELY TELL EACH OTHER EXACTLY HOW THEY FEEL. GO AHEAD, EAVESDROP—IT'S RESEARCH.

**DAWN RAFFEL**
AUTHOR OF *THE STRANGE CASE OF DR. COUNEY*

# 6

# DO YOUR HOMEWORK

My eleventh-grade English teacher, Mr. Peterson, was a repugnant little toad. He was small and scrazzy-haired. Late forties, going on CryptKeeper. If Ann Coulter and Bilbo Baggins got drunk and fornicated in the literary reference section of a state university library, the unholy fruit of that union would be Mr. Peterson.

Junior year, he made us write a forty-page paper on *Great Expectations*. That's the brand of unpasteurized evil I'm talking about here, people, but he got away with it, because this was a small Evangelical Lutheran high school where teachers were allowed to beat you with a stick, academically and literally. According to my Wisconsin Synod Lutheran education, the planet Earth is six thousand years old and anyone who doesn't get baptized in Jesus goes to Hell. (Sorry 'bout yer luck, Anne Frank, Gandhi, and stillborn babies.) The Holocaust was payback in that dogma, and English was all about the classics: lots of dead white men, sentence diagramming, and *Strunk & White's Elements of Style*.

I rarely did homework and barely scuttled by in other subjects, but I always got an A in English. For better or worse, I happened to love classics and diagramming sentences, and I had a serious nerd crush on Strunk & White. So with great confidence, I handed in my *Great Expectations* paper. A few weeks later, Petey handed the papers back, graded and degraded. I and my friend Greta, who'd been on the valedictorian track since kindergarten, had each gotten an A. There was an audible groan from the rest of the class.

Mr. Peterson made a few snide comments about the worst of the papers and then commenced the day's lesson, lecturing about something else. Suddenly, he stopped. Mid-sentence. He stood still for a long moment, balancing a stub of chalk on his palm. Then he walked over to my desk, seized my paper, crossed out the A and marked over it with a broad, red F.

Beneath it, he wrote, "You are such a clever writer, I almost believed you read this book."

*Doh!* I didn't bother trying to deny it. Petey allowed me to redo the paper with the highest possible grade being a C. Honestly, I was kind of stoked that he called me "clever," but as I came to understand the difference between *clever* and *intelligent*, I picked up on the side-eye.

Stephen King:

> **"IF YOU DON'T HAVE TIME TO READ, YOU DON'T HAVE THE TIME (OR THE TOOLS) TO WRITE. SIMPLE AS THAT."**

Not long after this, I was at my job, working the bar rush shift at a Denny's-type establishment called The Embers. To my horror, a group of teachers from Luther High rowdied in at about 3:00 a.m. Most of them were hammered and showed no chagrin about it when I approached with water and coffee—as if teachers had every right to carouse around partying all night. They gave me the usual hard time that drunks, who always think they're hilarious, always give waitresses, who know that serving drunks is more dignified than being one. I took their orders and went to prep their salads, and—

*What? No!*

Peterson, that wizened little warlock, followed me.

"You're not allowed to have a job until you're a senior," he said. "Do your parents know you're here?"

"Of course." I glanced nervously toward the night manager. Customers weren't supposed to be in the salad dressing area. Bad things happened in the salad dressing area.

"Why aren't you taking the SAT test tomorrow?" Peterson demanded.

"I am," I said. "Greta's picking me up here at seven."

"I'm sure you'll do well," he huffed, "seeing how you've applied yourself to preparing for it."

Mr. P returned to the table where my German teacher and our rotund principal had burst into an emotional rendition of "Ein Prosit." I dashed to the back room and called Greta to ask her if she could take me with her to the SAT test. At the end of my shift, she picked me up, and we went to a cold room at the university, where I took the test in my waitress uniform, reeking of bacon and sausage links.

Each day at Luther High began with "chapel," an assembly of the faculty and student body (only about four hundred kids) for the Pledge of Allegiance, a few stolid hymns, a dour sermon, prayers, and announcements. One morning several weeks after the SATs, the principal closed with an announcement that a Luther High student had received a letter of recognition from President Carter and an invitation to join Mensa, having scored in the top tenth of the top one percent nationally on the SATs.

People instinctively shuffled aside for Greta, who was beaming her homecoming queen smile. When the principal said my name, there was a silent thud of *WTF*, followed by a polite smattering of applause. Dying a thousand deaths, I went up and collected the letter and hid in the stage curtains until everyone had filed out of the gymnasium.

Just as an aside: I never saw the SAT score as proof that I was smart. I saw it as proof that standardized testing is a joke. Writers, as a species, are usually pretty clever, and many are able to take the "fake it till you make it" approach a long way in this business. But there comes a point where people expect you to meet deadlines and deliver the goods, which requires discipline, diligence, and respect for convention.

It came as a kick in the head for me when I started making money and writing became a job. A job as in work. It was an adjustment that took a few years, and it might have been easier if I'd developed some decent study habits in school—like Greta, who got her PhD and has gone far in the world.

I had English first period, right after chapel, and as I scuttled to my desk, Mr. Peterson knocked one Ichabod knuckle on the back of my head.

"Do your homework," he said. "And stop reading this trash."

He nicked a copy of Jacqueline Susann's *Once Is Not Enough* from my hand and chucked it into the circular file with a metallic clang. (The sound I hear every time I get a bad review.) He skewered me with a scornful gaze and said:

## "BEING SMART DOESN'T MEAN YOU CAN'T BE WORTHLESS. IT MEANS YOU CAN BE TRAGICALLY WORTHLESS."

To my consternation, the SAT score called attention to the fact that I was a remarkably poor student. Rather than take this as an indication that they were killing my soul, my teachers diagnosed a bad attitude, treatable with frequent stints in detention.

Adding insult to injury, I had Mr. Peterson for English again my senior year. The first day of class, we couldn't help but notice … his foot has been amputated. He never said a word about it, and we were too afraid of him to ask, but we heard through the grapevine that he had some kind of bone cancer.

When we came back from Thanksgiving break, his leg had ben taken off just below the knee. When we came back from Easter break, it was off at mid-thigh. Mr. Peterson withered to a winter twig and developed the thin, persistent cough of an elderly rat terrier. Still, he never said a word, and as I recall, never missed a day of class.

Toward spring, he introduced us to the poetry of Robert Herrick. Not the sexy stuff I still love to read. Cheerful monometers like:

*Thus I*

*Pass by*

*And die*

*As one*

*Unknown*

*And gone.*

More to my liking were the *carpe diem* "Gather ye rosebuds while ye may" poems and the lushly romantic love songs like "Upon Julia's Clothes":

*Whenas in silks my Julia goes*

*Then, then, methinks how sweetly flows*

*The liquefaction of her clothes…*

Mr. Peterson sucked all the joy out it, of course, saying that this was not about the woman at all; it's about her clothes, therefore not a soul-sending love poem, but a terse statement about superficiality and the distractions of fame. Herrick, it seems, never experienced the celebrity his contemporaries enjoyed, and Petey was righteously pissed off on the poet's behalf.

"But he says *my* Julia," I pointed out. "So either it's a love poem or he's admitting that deep down he wants to be a famous writer, too."

"He's mocking the fashion, the meaningless fads of publishing success. The word 'glittering'—that's not a loving word. It's hard. Sharp. It describes an object that has no light of its own, just a cheap, reflected flicker of glory. It's a deeply dissatisfied word."

"Well, he should have been grateful," I said tartly. "If he was a woman, he wouldn't have been published at all."

"Thank you, Erica Jong," Mr. Peterson clucked and rolled his eyes, handing out a mimeographed sheet, another example of a sestet, which he ordered me to read aloud.

Oh, how I wish I still had that mimeographed sheet. I don't remember anything about the poem except that it was labeled "by

Anonymous," and it was so achingly lovely, so filled with yearning, I stumbled at the end, a lump in my throat. I bit my trembling lip through a brief discussion of the sestet.

The bell rang. People shuffled their books and papers to go.

"You wrote it," I blurted.

Petey glared at me and clacked his crutch against the chalkboard.

"Anonymous." He barked a tattered cough into his skinny fist. "What part of anonymous do you not understand?"

In *I Know Why the Caged Bird Sings*, Maya Angelou writes:

> ## "THERE IS NO GREATER AGONY THAN BEARING AN UNTOLD STORY INSIDE YOU."

The frustration of unread writing is unrequited love to the tenth power.

I failed to graduate with my class, but I got my diploma that summer, and a few weeks into my first (and only) year of college, I saw Mr. Peterson for the last time.

I'd been at a late-night party that segued to early breakfast, so the sun was coming up as I stumbled out of McDonalds with my party peeps. There, to my dismay, was Rumpelstiltskin, sitting at my bus stop reading a weathered library book. There was nothing left of his leg now. Not much left of him. He was very obviously dying, and his distaste at seeing me was undisguised.

"Miss Lonnquist," he said, "what are you doing with your life?"

I chirped a bit about being a theatre major and moving to New York someday. I cringe thinking about it now, but I think I actually made the profoundly idiotic declaration, "Broadway is my biology!"

"The English language is part of your soul," he said. "If you don't write, it will be the greatest tragedy of your life."

Naturally, I blew that off. I was a wise woman of eighteen, and he was this old middle-aged guy.

Flash forward fourteen years.

It was very odd for me to think about old Petey as I felt bits and pieces of myself being carved away by cancer. How odd, I pondered; it seemed to be turning out that I was the one who was middle-aged when I was in high school.

As a child of the 1960s and '70s, I didn't know any cancer survivors. I knew people who'd come down with cancer and died, including my grandfather, this teacher, a friend's father, and one of my tenth-grade classmates, so I had no concept of what my life would be in the wake of it. As unpleasant as it was being in treatment, the bottomless pit of *what next?* was just as terrifying.

With damage to my heart and lung, I didn't have the stamina to even imagine myself doing theatre again. My throat was scarred from intubation and vomiting, so I no longer had the platinum pipes required for voiceovers. I wasn't brassy enough to call myself a writer just yet, but I must have had faith on some level that it was going to happen, because I kept at it.

Sherman Alexie:

> **"DO YOU KNOW WHY THE INDIAN RAIN DANCES ALWAYS WORKED? BECAUSE THE INDIANS WOULD KEEP DANCING UNTIL IT RAINED."**

It's probably a good thing I didn't know how truly farfetched it was, thinking I could get that first novel published. This book was everything a novel was not supposed to be: too commercial to be literary, too literary to be a romance, too romantic to be political, too political to be commercial, too commercial to be—you get my drift.

It wasn't worthless. It was *tragically* worthless.

In the handwritten rejection letters, I kept getting the word "quirky" and "neither fish nor fowl," and that, my darlings, is the kiss of death. I didn't know this then, but when an editor wants to acquire a book, s/he must run it through a committee meeting at which market-ing folk—who are overworked and underloved—want to know exactly which bookstore shelf is being targeted, and if there's no ready genre label, the editor better be backed up by a chorus of seraphim or forget it. While no one actually pointed to a "White Only" water fountain in so many words, there were several comments about a "cultural discon-nect" readers might feel about a Jewish heroine and Native American anti-hero. Half a dozen agents were honest enough to say, "I can't sell a book about a fat girl." The storyline about a bisexual secondary charac-ter was summed up as "a deal killer."

I stopped counting the rejections after about fifty, and as the last dozen or so trickled back to me, I stopped sending out queries to replace them. I found myself working less and less on the second novel, which was then titled *Blues Mommies*.

This was a pipe dream. I told myself to accept it.

Gary and I were desperately broke, and he was beginning to hint about me maybe getting some kind of job. Like a secretarial thing or something, since I'd gotten to be such a lightning-fast typist.

I packed up my manuscripts and dumped them out in the storage shed and sat in front of the TV day after day for the next few months, paralyzed with depression. I'd get the kids off to school in the morning and then lie on the floor in Malachi's room, playing "Dr. Robotnik's Mean Bean Machine" until it was time to meet the school bus in the afternoon. As the bright colored bubbles dribbled down the screen, Herrick tapped a bony knuckle at the back of my head.

*Thus I*
*Pass by*
*And die*
*As one*
*Unknown*
*And gone.*

# THEY SAY THE LORD NEVER GIVES US MORE THAN WE CAN BEAR. THIS IS TRUE ONLY OF MONEY AND CLEAVAGE.

It came to pass that spring that the Lord let loose one of the prodigious Houston downpours that make us look like Haiti on the Weather Channel. That stupid storage shed flooded, and I had to drag myself out there to clean it up. As I picked up a soggy cardboard box, its bottom flaps gave way, and a beautiful depression glass piggy bank my grandmother had given me smashed on the floor.

Among the scattered pennies and broken glass, I saw a piece of paper. A corner torn from a McDonald's placemat. On the back of it was written, "The English language is part of your soul, and if you don't write, it'll be the greatest tragedy of your life."

It was my own handwriting—the teenage version—but I had no memory of writing that down or tucking it in the piggy bank. But I did vividly remember that morning at the bus stop. My teacher sat there dying, with no evidence that he'd made the slightest impact on my life, no reason to suspect that fifteen years later, his words would come back to me like a life raft.

But not like a teacher's words to a student. At eighteen, I was too feckless to know it, but he was speaking to me as one writer to another.

"The greatest tragedy of your life," he said, and he knew this for a fact, because it was the greatest tragedy of his. I suspect Mr. Peterson realized a little too late that, yes, Marlo Thomas, we are all special in our own way, but only a few of us are special in *this* way. And whatever way you are special in, you owe it to the universe and to yourself to get off your ass and do something with it.

I rescued my manuscripts, picked up where I'd left off on the second novel and cranked up my query rotation again.

Don't play "Eye of the Tiger" just yet. I was still depressed as hell. Every fresh rejection felt like a boot to the kidney. But I stopped counting them. The number was irrelevant.

# REJECTION IS USEFUL AS A STEPPINGSTONE, NOT A STUMBLING BLOCK.

I learned what I could from anyone kind enough to comment, accepted the criticism that resonated, blew off the rest, ever mindful of Isaac Asimov's famous two-word answer to being asked what he would do if he knew he had one day to live:

"Type faster."

Out of seventy or eighty queries, I'd had only a handful of requests for the full manuscript. As I limped down to the last few dollars I could justifiably spend on this endeavor, with nothing to lose, I tried a small experiment: I sent out my last dozen queries with the identical query package I'd been using since I started the rotation, but I changed my name from Joni Rodgers to J. R. Rodgers.

Within two weeks, all but one of the publishers came back with requests for the full manuscript. All eleven requests began "Dear Mr. Rodgers."

Whatever. I was too elated to be outraged. I felt genuinely hopeful for the first time, but I didn't have enough money to send out all those manuscripts.

I sent out two.

Both publishers came back with offers on the book. I accepted a contract with MacMurray & Beck, a small but prestigious literary press that later merged with MacAdam-Cage. The advance was $4,000, and in light of our financial woes, Griz and I did the responsible thing and used the money to take our kids to Disney World.

Cue "Eye of the Tiger."

I can't begin to count how many times I've been told it was impossible to place a novel—or get a ghostwriting gig—without an agent. I've done both, so I'm not afraid to be without an agent. I do believe in the power of advocacy; I have a great agent now, and she's changed my life. But I've had a few bad experiences that taught me something

I never would have accepted back in the early days when I just wanted someone—anyone—to take me on.

**HAVING THE RIGHT AGENT IS A HUGE STEP UP. HAVING THE WRONG AGENT IS WORSE THAN HAVING NO AGENT AT ALL.**

Keeping all that in mind, turn the page for an informal step-by-step strategy for vetting and connecting with the right agent for you. Remember that this is an equal business partnership. You are not a beggar; you can be a chooser.

# AGENT QUERY

# STRATEGY CHECKLIST

1. Clarify your objectives:
   - What do you have ready to sell right now?
     - Describe in 100 words
     - Describe in 10 words
   - What kind of publisher are you trying to reach?
     - Genre/literary
     - Big 6/small press
   - What are your short and long-term goals for this project?
     - Max advance
     - Flex advance w higher back end
     - Tangible intangibles (platform, traction, etc.)
   - What are your goals for author/agent relationship?
     - Help you craft a career
     - Place a specific book project
     - Broker co-author arrangements
   - Are you looking for a corporate or boutique agency?
   - What sort of agency agreement are you willing to sign?
2. Vet agents via Publishers Marketplace:
   - WHAT HAS THIS AGENT SOLD RECENTLY?
   - Do you like their general vibe?
   - Who else do they rep?
   - How long have they been in the biz?
   - What are their submission policies?
3. Craft the contact package:
   - The Hallowed Query Letter
     - 300 words max
     - Personal greeting

- o Who are you?
- o What is the project in hand?
- o What are you attaching?
- o What are you ready to send on request?
- o Contact info
- o "Thank you for your time and interest."
- Attach at least one powerful writing sample
  - o Attach as Word doc
  - o Double space
  - o Times New Roman 12 pt
  - o No images/fancy fonts/embellishments
  - o 2500—3500 words

4. Follow up:
   - If it's a flat no/form rejection
     - o THANK YOU

   - If it's a request for more material
     - o PROMPTLY fire off full ms with NO excuses/ disclaimers
     - o THANK YOU

   - If it's a request to chat on the phone
     - o THANK YOU
     - o Wooooot!

   - On the call:
     - o Be professional
     - o Be yourself
     - o Ask a lot of questions

**THE TRICK IS NOT BECOMING
A WRITER. THE TRICK IS
STAYING A WRITER.**

HARLAN ELLISON
AUTHOR OF *I HAVE NO MOUTH
AND I MUST SCREAM*

**WRITING, AT ITS BEST, IS A LONELY LIFE. ORGANIZATIONS FOR WRITERS PALLIATE THE WRITER'S LONELINESS, BUT I DOUBT IF THEY IMPROVE HIS WRITING. HE GROWS IN PUBLIC STATURE AS HE SHEDS HIS LONELINESS, AND OFTEN HIS WORK DETERIORATES. FOR HE DOES HIS WORK ALONE, AND IF HE IS A GOOD ENOUGH WRITER HE MUST FACE ETERNITY, OR THE LACK OF IT, EACH DAY.**

ERNEST HEMINGWAY
AUTHOR OF *THE SUN ALSO RISES*

# 7

# STAY CRAZY

One of the insanely frustrating things about this business is that every time you think you've arrived, you quickly discover you haven't. I thought getting my first novel published meant that I was now a novelist. Someone who could make a living writing novels. But after *Crazy for Trying* came out, the publisher turned down my second novel, and that editor, though he remains my friend, has never again been interested in publishing me. I no longer fit in as a member of that small literary press coterie. I'm not sure I ever did.

I confess, this makes me feel bad, even when I remind myself that the advances suck. It's like an exquisitely posh dinner party at which only lima beans are served. You're not really missing much, but it still hurts to not be invited because you know a lot of cool people are there.

Back to the query rotation.

Swamped with pharmaceuticals, living in immune-compromised isolation, I immersed myself in the sort of books you read when you think you're dying. *Till We Have Faces* by C. S. Lewis, a philosophical retelling of the Psyche and Eros myth, blew my mind and prompted a Bullfinch reading binge. A dark dramedy took shape in my head as I thought about how the complicated story of Psyche and her extended family might play if I dropped it into my world—a working class suburb in Houston, Texas—with full advantage of melodic Southern dialect and over-the-top Southern family dynamics.

My second novel, *Sugarland*, is a modern reimagining of my favorite myth: "What if Psyche and Eros had been southeast Texas trailer trash?" Most of it was written on yellow legal pads as I sat for long hours tied to an IV tree at the infusion clinic. I'd fallen completely in love with the Southern dialect and was searching for creative pockets into which I could stuff some of the overwhelming emotions of mid-chemo motherhood. The novel is structured in trimesters, like a pregnancy, and in many ways, it felt like I was giving birth to my writer self as I worked through the first draft.

With brilliant editing from Joan Drury, *Sugarland* was published in 1999 by Spinsters Ink, a feisty little feminist press based in Duluth, Minnesota, and later by Bertelsmann, the parent company of Random House, in Europe. It did well, won a few awards, and got good reviews. The German translation, *Fast wei im Paradies*, was a bestseller and generated hundreds of letters, which was trippy, even though I had no idea if they were fan or hate mail.

Best of all, *Sugarland* had a nice run with book clubs all over the United States; I was lucky enough to sit in on more than a hundred robust, wine-fueled discussions at bookstores, bars, and in readers' homes—an eye-opening privilege I've not had with any other book. Even in 2001, when I was touring to promote my memoir, *Bald in the Land of Big Hair*, many book clubs I visited wanted to go back and rehash their previous year's conversation about *Sugarland*. The story of Kit and Kiki turned out to be a vehicle for polarized, revealing conversations about how endemic sexism and misogyny haven't changed that much over the past three thousand years, particularly when it comes to casual language and shaming qualifiers attached to sexual assault and domestic violence.

Lord, I wish this book would stop being so fucking relevant.

Kit and Kiki are caught up in the type of dreams and frustrations quickly understood by most young mothers. Kit's husband Mel is a gentle salt-of-the-earth working man; Kiki's husband Wayne is the golden son of a privileged family—a man whose good looks and charm mask a terrifying mean streak. The complex arc of the story arises from an incident revealed in succinct emotional and physical detail close to the beginning of the book: Kit is raped by Wayne. Later in the book,

Wayne violently beats and rapes his wife, and the language purposely echoes the rape of Kit, which is less physically violent but no less monstrous. Both assaults are clearly about power, not sex.

The damage done to Kit as her children and her sister's children are sleeping on the floor just a few feet away takes her into Psyche's perilous realm. She loses herself to shame and denial and methodically destroys her own life. In the midst of that desperate downward spiral, Kit has a comforting sexual encounter with Ander, her longtime friend and employer. Again, the language was carefully constructed to demonstrate the difference between the rape and this situation in which Kit is a willing participant.

But here's the thing about carefully constructed language:

## IT'S NOT ABOUT WHAT THE WRITER WRITES; IT'S ABOUT WHAT THE READER READS.

From a review in Library Journal (emphasis mine): "When both sisters become pregnant for the third time, suffering ensues: cataclysmic loss for Kiki and overwhelming guilt for Kit, unsure of her unborn child's paternity after **a virtual assault** by Wayne and a spontaneous tumble with her boss."

Ponder with me the problematic false equivalence of "virtual assault" and "spontaneous tumble"—or the problematic notion that "virtual assault" is even a thing.

From *Publishers Weekly*: "Meanwhile, **Kit has two quickie flings**, resulting in a pregnancy of questionable paternity. Readers with true equality of the sexes on their minds may object that **Kiki's husband's cheating is treated as an actionable offense while Kit's marital excursions are permitted the luxury of mitigating circumstances.**"

Quickie. Fling.

I physically cough-barked when I saw that. At least the "marital excursion" enjoyed the "luxury of mitigating circumstances." Because getting raped is a *luxury*, you see. 'Cause then you have a good excuse when you explain yourself to the satisfaction of—*gah!* Whatever.

These are two reviews among many that had high praise for the book itself but proved the book's point with semantic bet-hedging over whether it really counts as rape if a woman wasn't adequately beaten before, during, or after she was forcibly penetrated. The assumption is that Kit—unhappy in her tepid marriage—was consciously or subconsciously asking for it. And what a feminazi I was for treating poor Wayne's "cheating" as an "actionable offense"!

Note to anyone doing jury duty: *IT IS.*

When I visited book clubs, which were populated overwhelmingly by women readers, I was astounded to find that discussions often centered, at least in part, on what Kit could have and should have done to prevent the rape from happening. And we wonder why 90 percent of sexual assaults go unreported.

When I told Joan Drury about these book club conversations, she said:

> **"NOW YOU KNOW WHY THIS BOOK IS IMPORTANT. THEY'RE HAVING THE CONVERSATION. THEY'RE TALKING ABOUT IT. THAT'S A VICTORY."**

It was a difficult lesson to ingest—this idea that writers don't get to be the puppet master in a reader's brain—but what I took from it was freedom. I let go of my attachment to a specific audience reaction, and that liberated me to tell stories I believe in, however I choose to tell them.

While *Sugarland* was in the pipeline, I wrote my memoir, *Bald in the Land of Big Hair*. I'd gotten no advance at all for Sugarland, but that meant it started earning royalties right away. *Sugarland* was fairy-godmothered by Claire Kirch and a few other amazing women at Spinsters, who fished in some great reviews for it and sold foreign rights to Bertelsmann, an overseas publishing behemoth. Stellar reviews for *Sugarland* attracted the attention of my first literary agent, who sold the memoir to HarperCollins. *Bald in the Land of Big Hair* also got great reviews and was condensed for both *Good Housekeeping* and *Reader's Digest*, so now I was immortalized on the backs of toilets from sea to shining sea. For my parents, this meant I had truly arrived. I had made it.

But the thing is, in publishing—as in life—there's no such thing. "Made it" is a wishfully past tense concept that pretends there's some magical place where it all becomes easy, where respect is a given, where the grind will be less grueling. Dear reader, that is not a thing. In more than one low moment, I've described the writing life, borrowing the words of Jerry Maguire:

> ## "IT IS AN UP-AT-DAWN, PRIDE-SWALLOWING SIEGE THAT I WILL NEVER FULLY TELL YOU ABOUT."

I'm not sure any of us really grok what we're getting into. And that's probably healthy.

HarperCollins had an option on my third novel, and they eventually picked it up, but it wasn't published until five years later, and it was the biggest bellyflop of my career. My original title for this book was *The Prodigal Wife*, and I wish I'd been stronger when I was pressured to change it. My editor didn't force me; in fact, she scolded me for being "such an orphan in the storm" when it came to sticking up for myself. Suffering from what Oprah Winfrey calls "the disease to please," I was eager to do whatever my industry betters told me I should do, thinking that would secure my place in the corporate sugar daddy's affections. The publisher had an option on my next novel, and my editor introduced me to a fabulous literary agent who brought me into a prestigious New York stable. I was really taken with talk of this chichi agency and mega-house being my "publishing home" for the rest of my career. In light of all that, the title change seemed like a relatively small thing, but I ended up deeply regretting it.

This novel was a bit of a departure from my previous work. I've always been a happy and optimistic person by nature—I still am—but this story is definitely more tragedy than comedy. It's darker, more erotic, and more message-driven than anything else I'd written. The agoraphobic protagonist is fleeced by a con artist. Her party girl sister goes to jail for vehicular homicide after killing their niece in a drunk driving incident. Their bereaved sister-in-law is forced to confront the fact that the dead child she's reinvented as a cherub was actually a little wretch who was more than somewhat responsible for her own death. Each of these women serves hard time in a prison of her own making before she finds redemption.

## MY PRIME DIRECTIVE IS ALWAYS TO TELL A GREAT STORY.

But I wanted this to be a deeper, more thought-provoking parable about what we sacrifice when we embrace fear as a lifestyle. It's about the art of manipulation, the craft of seduction, and the blissful but dangerous state of denial. It's also about empowerment and accountability.

In *Crazy for Trying*, fire is a symbol of self-destructive passions. In *Sugarland*, I used tornadoes as a metaphor for the centripetal force of a mother's love. In *The Prodigal Wife*, I had the brilliant (I wish) idea to use sexual manipulation as an analogy in my stinging (I thought) indictment of post-9/11 fear mongering.

Sam Goldwyn:

## "IF YOU WANT TO SEND A MESSAGE, USE WESTERN UNION."

A lot of people found the book offensive, some because of the lefty politics but most because of the graphic sexual content. One outraged consumer wrote, "You are sick sick SICK! After reading this book several times, I still can't believe how disgusting it is!"

As the Griz watched me dig out from under an avalanche of hate mail calling me a pornographer, slut, anal sex fiend, and bad, bad BAD writer, he suggested that maybe the title should be changed yet again to give folks more of a heads up about the dodgy parts. His suggestion: *The Dirty, Dirty Dildo Sex Book*, which he promptly shortened to DDDSB. Anagrams often facilitate teasing at Chez Rodgers.

The old "sex sells" concept rarely holds true in literary fiction, particularly if a woman writes it. We could go back and forth for hours about what is actually sexy or not sexy when set to words, but beyond that is the question of the purpose of sex in a story, and even when the purpose is character development or plot advance, it's often doomed, not because of the way it's written, but because of the way it's read.

I call it The Godiva Factor.

The real Lady Godiva was the beautiful wife of Leofric, Earl of Mercia, one of the most powerful noblemen in eleventh-century England. She was much younger than her husband and used her influence on him to divert support to the arts and religious orders, hoping to raise the consciousness of the common folks. In 1043, Godiva and Leofric founded an Abbey in Coventry. The town grew. Leofric initiated ambitious public works projects and levied taxes to support them. Suffering under the burden, the locals had little interest in aesthetics, so Godiva pleaded with her husband to reduce taxes.

According to legend, Leofric sarcastically pointed out that the ancient Greeks and Romans viewed the nude human body as a high expression of nature's beauty. So if she really wanted to crusade for the sake of art, she could bloody well ride naked through the marketplace at midday, and if she did, he would abolish all local taxes except those on horses. Much to everyone's surprise, she did it. Flanked by two horsewomen (fully clothed), with noble posture and an expression of dignity and calm, she rode naked through the town of Coventry, and the taxes were repealed.

Or so the legend says.

If it's true, this was a courageous and selfless gesture, an incredibly bold political statement. If it's not true, the story likely sprang up because of other courageous, selfless, and incredibly bold things Lady Godiva did. But what is she remembered for? What do we think when we hear the words "Lady Godiva"? We think naked. Naked lady! *Ah-OO-gah!* She is the icon for nothing but nothing on. How revealing.

While most readers readily see fire and wind as metaphors, they tend to see two characters closing in, and everything goes gibberish until they fall back and light a cigarette before emailing you about what a pagan anal-sexing whore you are.

Not for a moment am I saying the failure of this book constitutes a failure on the part of readers. There are plenty of books that simply don't froogaloo with my personal filters or work for me as a reader. *All the Pretty Horses*, for example. I wanted to go there. I was willing. I'm smart enough, but dang it, I can't get comfortable with the lack of quotation marks. The readership I bring to a book just doesn't work with that. So I have to respect that the readership others bring to my books is equally willing and smart, but it's not always going to work with what I write.

If this novel had gone through the rigorous shaking and sifting of a great critique group, I might have been alerted to the fact that only one in a hundred readers would get it. My editor happened to be that one, and she supported my vision, God love her, pushing me to the highest literary standards of anything I'd ever written. Even people who despised the book had to admit it was very well written. I learned a lot from this editor, who became a dear friend, and that almost made the ensuing horse-whipping worth it.

Almost.

Looking back, I can honestly say I wouldn't change it. Lady Godiva knew exactly what she was risking, and so did I. Title change aside, that book says exactly what I wanted to say. It's good art.

# GOOD ART SOMETIMES MAKES PEOPLE UNCOMFORTABLE.

So do dildos and anal sex, apparently. Personally, I'm uncomfortable with Karl Rove, institutionalized torture, and unnecessary wars. We all have our little hang-ups.

But, I feel ya, Lady G. Maybe, I'm her one in a hundred. When I hear the name Godiva, I don't think *naked*. I don't even think naked *chocolate*. I think art. I think *courage*. I think *revolution*.

"I said exactly what I wanted to say," I told my agent. "Given the chance, I'd do it again."

But in this business, you don't always get another chance. In terms of literary quality, the DDDSB is probably the best thing I've ever written, thanks in part to my brilliantly strict editor, but it was a personal and professional disaster that changed the course of my career.

One evening I had dinner with my editor and her husband in New York, and over cocktails, she resolutely told me, "You have talent. Keep working hard. When your next book comes out, no one will remember this."

I went home feeling fortified. I was still in love with the idea of my prestigious "publishing home," and tremendously grateful for the time and energy my editor was devoting to my next novel.

The next night, her husband drunk-dialed me. His awkward excuse for calling quickly segued to the sexually explicit passages in my novel. One passage in particular. He wanted me to read it to him. I nervously laughed off the request and tried to give us both a face-saving exit from the conversation, but he became insistent. I bluntly told him it was not going to happen and ended the call. He called back. I answered, hoping he was calling back to say it was all a misunderstanding. He wasn't. I quickly ended the call. The phone rang again. I didn't answer.

I called Gary at work, and he was disgusted and nonplussed. He offered to call the guy, but I didn't want to escalate things. I decided it would be best to try to ignore it. I closed my office door, crawled into bed and lay there with a knot in my gut, listening to the phone ring late into the night.

First thing in the morning, I called my agent. His emphatic advice: "Never. Tell. Anyone." And I never did until years later.

"Just pretend it didn't happen," said my agent. "Hopefully, he won't remember it."

I tried to keep my eye on the prize, as they say, but the next day, I felt horribly uncomfortable being on the phone with my editor, and she could tell. She asked me if I was upset with her about the title change, and I assured her I wasn't, but after that, I tried to keep communications about the developing option novel going on email.

A few weeks later, my editor heard from a colleague that I was in New York working on a ghostwriting project, and she sent me an email suggesting I have dinner with her and her husband again. With my heart in my throat, I tried to compose a casual reply, making a credible excuse to get out of it. But before I had a chance to click SEND, I got another email from her:

"My husband just reminded me we have other plans."

There was a sea change in my career over the next few months. My editor stopped answering my emails and abruptly pulled the plug on development of the option novel. Then my agent—a good friend of the editor—dropped me. I found myself with no publisher and no representation, negotiating my own guerrilla ghostwriting gigs under the table. The most painful aspect of it all was the loss of my relationship with my editor, a fabulous mentor who'd taught me so much and meant so much to me as a friend. It was a long time before I heard from her. We never spoke on the phone again. Our sporadic emails over the years were a friendly but distant exchange confined to the business of books we had in common. When I heard through the grapevine that she had died, it felt like stepping on a spike of broken glass.

Over the years, I regretted the title change and other compromises I'd made on the DDDSB. But more than the failure of the book, I was troubled by my failure to stand up for my creative choices, call out the spouse's shitty behavior, and tell that agent to shove his "never tell" advice up his ass.

At this writing, it's out of print, and I'm trying to get the rights back so I can restore it and release it as an indie, because I still believe in the book itself. I'm still proud of it.

Back then, my swank literary agent warned me that if I didn't make the title change, I would be branded "difficult"—and I wonder if he gives his male authors that same advice—but after he cut me loose, I resolved: every choice I make from here forward will be something for which I am wholeheartedly willing to go down in flames. Going down in flames for anything less is too bitter a pill, no matter how sweet the incentive. If that brands me as difficult, I'll proudly wear the word.

With Gary's Rock of Gibraltar job and my sporadic ghost gigs keeping us afloat, I went back to the query routine, trying to get another agent, but predictably, the first two questions everyone asked were: "Didn't you just change agents a few months ago?" and "Why isn't your current publisher picking up the option on your novel?"

I had no answer.

## PUBLISHING IS A VERY SMALL TOWN.

Gossip is gold, and I didn't want that story going around. My editor didn't deserve to be hurt or humiliated by her husband's creepy behavior, and for my own sake, I didn't want that to be the thing people talked about when my name came up in conversation. I was trying hard to look like a novelist who was still viable on my own steam.

The sad fact is, I wasn't, because in the old caste system, authors were only as viable as their agent and publisher allowed them to be. We were the supplicants, lucky to be in if and when they said we were in and categorically out the moment they said we were out. With hoards of aspiring writers pressing their noses to the glass, agents and editors were the omnipotent gatekeepers who kept the riffraff away from the delicate sensibilities of readers, and readers widely believed that the gatekeeping criterion was about artistic merit more than it was about money or cronyism. Public perception was that published authors were good and unpublished authors sucked—which was a misperception at best, and at worst, an insurmountable, suicide-tempting wall of despair for a huge number of very fine artists.

In the decade leading up to the digital publishing revolution, the enormous imbalance of power had become ridiculously toxic to authors and a grave disservice to readers. It was unhealthy for the body literati as an organic ecosystem.

This isn't a stinging indictment of publishers and agents. Publishing is a business, not a charity, though it does sometimes act on altruistic motives. Agents are salespeople, not missionaries, though they do occasionally tilt at windmills for their own noble reasons.

## AUTHORS ARE RESPONSIBLE FOR STANDING UP FOR THE VALUE OF OUR WORK.

For too long, too many authors happily snuggled up to the old sugar daddy system where we were alternately flattered and spanked, taken care of and taught to behave.

Within that business model, writing careers could and did fail for a variety of reasons that had nothing to do with the quality of the author's work. Maybe the author's agent had a nervous breakdown or an editor suffered a stroke and a book was orphaned on an abandoned desk. Maybe the marketing team was out to lunch or the cover designer missed the mark. Maybe the author failed to comply with the inclinations of someone with influence to wield. I'm certainly not the only author—female or male—who's been creeped on, and I certainly wasn't the only midlist author who found herself out in the cold as the economy crumbled in 2008, taking the publishing industry with it.

With advances shrinking and the Bookscan garrote around our necks, many of us were rudely awakened to the cold, hard truth:

# IF THE SUGAR DADDY'S OUT OF MONEY, HONEY, YOU'RE JUST GETTING SCREWED.

**MY DEATH AND LIFE,
MY BANE AND ANTIDOTE
ARE BOTH BEFORE ME.**

JOSEPH ADDISON
AUTHOR OF *CATO, A TRAGEDY*

# HOW'S THAT WORKING OUT?

Writing and querying are both about process, and process requires planning. Take a quick action/expectation inventory below.

My overall goal as a writer:

What I've done in the past twelve months to achieve my goal:

- Action:
  - o Results:

- Action:
  - o Results:

- Action:
  - o Results:

What I can do in the coming twelve months to achieve my goal:

- Action:
  - o Expectation:

- Action:
  - o Expectation:

- Action:
  - o Expectation:

**SOFT AS SOME
SONG DIVINE
THY STORY FLOWS.**

HOMER
AUTHOR OF *THE ODYSSEY*

# 8

# YOU'VE GOT TO HAVE FRIENDS

Before my agent dumped me, she told me a critical and commercial disaster like this would probably preclude me from ever writing fiction under my own name again, and I was actually okay with that for a while. Ghostwriting had shown me that seeing my name on the cover of the book was not nearly as rewarding as seeing the book on a bookshelf. Or even a bestseller list. I dated a series of nom de plumes, made a semi-serious commitment to one, and applied it to a couple of mystery novels that went nowhere.

One day, when my cash reserves were almost gone, I stopped and picked up a job application at a Mexican restaurant where I'd seen a "Dishwasher Wanted" sign. I owe it to Gary to pull my share of the load, but I didn't want a job that would require me to spend money on wardrobe or take up any of the mental real estate I needed for the novel I was working on.

The application stayed on a bulletin board in my office as a reminder for the next twenty years. It's all I have to fall back on, so it's all I need to spur me on.

What truly saved my sanity during those years was my critique group, the Midwives.

I was officing in the coffee shop at Borders one Friday afternoon, and bestselling romantic suspense author Colleen Thompson happened to be doing a table signing. You know how table signings are. Painfully uneventful events where an author sits like a big-eyed pound puppy at a wooden table near the entrance of Barnes & Noble. Because I personally feel table signings are the seventh circle of hell, I don't walk past one without buying a book and chatting up the author, but I found Colleen working her table signing with a great attitude and steady sales.

While Colleen and I were talking, one of her critique mates, women's fiction author Barbara (Bobbi) Taylor Sissel, walked over and joined the small talk, which evolved to a chat fest, which ended up with me being in the Midwives with Colleen, Bobbi, Wanda Dionne, who'd been published as a YA author before she genre-hopped to write suspense, and T.J. Bennett, who's been published in historical romance and as a ghostwriter.

When emerging authors ask me for advice, the first thing I tell them is to find a great critique group. If you can't find one, create one. Nowadays, with Zoom, Teams, and the ever-evolving work-at-home accomodations, the possibilities are unlimited. You don't want to be the smartest one in the group. (I definitely don't need to worry about that.)

## EACH OF YOU SHOULD BRING SOMETHING TO THE TABLE THAT NO ONE ELSE DOES.

The brilliant Midwives are a gift in both my professional and personal life. We're good friends, but we're all in the business when we sit down together every other Friday night. We each bring ten pages, which we read aloud, holding comments until the end. No punches are pulled, but affirmation isn't stingy. Colleen has a gentle approach she describes as "two to glow and one to grow." The caliber of the peer editing in this group makes us all look a lot better in front of our editors and agents, who rarely see anything that hasn't been properly vetted by the group.

Beyond that is an emotional support system that isn't possible from non-writer friends, sisters, and significant others. Each of us has felt the sting of rejection and the euphoria of acceptance. We understand why the thought of changing agents makes you want to curl up in a ball under your desk. We forgive each other for bad moments and promote each other in the marketplace. We get the jokes. We eat dessert. Coffee, chocolate, and candor are applied as needed.

## SOLITUDE IS A GIFT AND CURSE FOR WRITERS.

Do not—do *not*, my darlings—attempt to cure it with Facebook. Make real connections. Find fantastic critique partners. And don't lose touch with the friends who don't understand anything about publishing. They keep you anchored to the real world of readers.

In *Talk Before Sleep*, Elizabeth Berg wrote, "The truth is, we usually only show our unhappiness to another woman. I suppose this is one of our problems. And yet it is also one of our strengths." Replace "another woman" with "another writer" and apply as needed to publishing and life.

**THERE ARE DAYS WHEN SOLITUDE IS A HEADY WINE THAT INTOXICATES YOU WITH FREEDOM,** OTHERS WHEN IT IS A BITTER TONIC, AND STILL OTHERS WHEN IT IS A POISON THAT MAKES YOU BEAT YOUR HEAD AGAINST THE WALL.

SIDONIE GABRIELLE COLETTE
AUTHOR OF *GIGI*

# WHO YA GONNA CALL?

Family. Friends. Ride-or-die writer bitches. Critique group. Mentors. Paid professional editors. Everyone has a role to play, and bless their hearts, but it's up to you to identify what you need, when you need it, and who you need it from. Create your call list below:

For a good time, call ________________________________________

because ______________________________________________

For unconditional encouragement, call ________________________

because ______________________________________________

For searingly honest critique, call __________________________

because ______________________________________________

For decompression and coffee, call __________________________

because ______________________________________________

For tech support, call ____________________________________

because ______________________________________________

For creative consult, call _________________________________

because ______________________________________________

**YOU DO NOT ACHIEVE ANYTHING WITHOUT TROUBLE. EVER.**

MARGARET ATWOOD
AUTHOR OF *THE HANDMAID'S TALE*

**9**

# BE OPEN

The year after *Bald in the Land of Big Hair* came out, my agent called to ask if I'd be interested in working on a book with a celebrity's mom. I'd never thought about ghostwriting and had no idea how that might be done, so I was about to say no—I was literally mid-syllable—when I saw a hummingbird outside my window. I'd been looking out that window for years and never seen one before.

It caused me to pause just long enough for my agent to say, "Have lunch with her and see what you think."

So we had lunch, and I liked her. She had a wonderful story, and I'm a storyteller, so I let the story lead the way. Apparently, this is a marketable skill, and in general, I love the collaborative process. The frustrations are many, but the rewards are huge. The money's excellent, but the greatest benefit for me has been working in the trenches with so many fantastically interesting people. I feel like I've been privately schooled and awarded a wheels-on-the-ground masters degree in show biz, music, and politics.

Through my extraordinary clients, I've been exposed to backstage, backlot, and boardroom worlds I never would have glimpsed otherwise. I always want them to feel creative ownership of their projects, so I coach them to write as much as possible. I've discovered that I love editing almost as much as I love writing, and thanks to my editor/tutors, I've gotten good at it.

Writing is like painting; editing is like sculpture.

Same sensibilities, different skill set.

Whatever you've written in the past, published or not, was an important step toward the next sentence you lay down. When you kill your darlings during the editing process, know that every word had to happen in order for you to find the real story.

## NO WORDS ARE WASTED, BUT SOME ARE PROCESS, NOT PRODUCT.

Seeing them as such makes it easier to liposuction words that get in the way.

Kibitzing back and forth with a writer friend one evening, I tried to explain the mindset that makes it possible for me to write books for which other people receive credit. It doesn't bother me to fade into the wallpaper. Fame was never high on my list of reasons for writing. In fact, it's never been on the list at all. Old Herrick had it right: it's a distraction, and I've hung around with famous people enough to see its corrosive effects.

I've had many such conversations over the years, and responses vary from "How do I get a gig like that?" to a variety of comments that boil down to "Whore! Whore of the Medicis!" The most common theme seems to be a disbelief that I could possibly be okay with it and a bit of an eye-roll when I, a lowly ghostwriter, aspire to high artistic ideals.

## ARTISTIC INTEGRITY IS SOMETHING I BRING TO THE PROJECT; I DON'T EXPECT THE PROJECT TO BESTOW IT ON ME.

For many writers, a major part of the thrill of being published is seeing one's name on the cover of a book. The author photo in the newspaper, a big poster announcing the table signing at Barnes & Noble, 2.5 minutes of fame on the *Today Show*—these are daydreams a lot of authors suck on like Tootsie Pops, not knowing that the best part is way below that hard sugar surface. For my first few books, I was totally on that bus. Loved getting out there and talking to people, meeting booksellers and doing interviews. It was trippy seeing my picture in the *London Daily Mail* and my face on the *Today Show*. I won't deny it. But that buzz wore thin when *The Prodigal Wife* belly-flopped. I held my ground in the tsunami of bad reviews and hate mail. I did a few humbling book events where people stayed away in droves and a few exhausting book club visits where everyone debated which character they hated most: the protagonist, the antagonist, or me for writing the thing.

Thrill. Gone.

I felt exposed and vulnerable, and my response to that was to pull into the safe, solid turtle shell of my home office. And I liked it. The necessary evil of self-promotion is a topic of much debate among authors. There's a healthy, keep-it-classy balance we all seek, but no one seems to know what the rules are for that. One thing that can be agreed on: it takes a lot of time and energy. If you're building a career as a novelist, that is time and energy well spent.

> ## I DISCOVERED THAT I WROTE A LOT MORE—AND A LOT BETTER—WHEN MY FOCUS WAS INWARD INSTEAD OF OUTWARD.

I realized that with ghostwriting, I'd drawn the *Get Out of PR Free* card. I could do the work I loved and have the big book-deal money without the soul-consuming project of being famous. For me, that is a quick and easy trade. The people who matter—editors and agents who bring me these interesting projects—all know that I'm the one doing the heavy lifting, not the celeb. I worked hard to build a solid rep as someone who has talent, meets deadlines, and gets along well with complicated people leading complicated lives.

I'd be a lousy journalist, because I believe the best willingly and the worst reluctantly. My mantra when I'm working on a celeb memoir is: *Gotta love her.* If I don't love this person, how will the reader love her? When I'm working with someone who is particularly difficult, my mantra is: *God, help me love this wounded child.* I can't help loving them as I learn their lives, their vulnerabilities. I know—because I've done a memoir of my own—that the memoir process can be emotionally grueling. If it isn't, you're probably not doing it right.

A memoir has only a skiff of a whiff in common with a biography. It's a totally different art form focused on reflection and introspection, not a recitation of details—though it is important to get the details right. I love this form because I love humans in all their flawed and fabulous glory. We the Reader need the memoir form to be human and soft and forgiving. Wouldn't you rather see a beautiful nude painted by Matisse as opposed to a stark, naked body web-cammed on a porn site? The Matisse is more subjective, yes, and that's what makes it a more accurate portrayal of who that person truly is in essence.

The key to being a successful ghostwriter is a complete suspension of vanity that enables one to genuinely love the project and the client for exactly what it is and who they are. If you go into it as a way to hobnob with the rich and famous, you're doomed, because they can smell that a mile off. If you go into it for the money, you're doomed, because it's unsteady and leads you into temptation; greed lures you to take projects you're not right for, and that is the road to ruin.

## ENTER INTO IT FOR THE SAKE OF THE BOOK. OR STAY HOME.

According to the dictionary:
**gestalt** \gə- ˈstält, - ˈshtält, - ˈstȯlt, - ˈshtȯlt
*Function: noun*
*Etymology: German, literally, shape, form*

*1: a structure, configuration, or pattern of physical, biological, or psychological phenomena so integrated as to constitute a functional unit with properties not derivable by summation of its parts*

There are several things people hate/disrespect about what ghost-writers do, and it's fruitless for me to try to defend one facet or another, because I see the gestalt. Is it cool for one person to take credit for another person's work? No, generally speaking, it isn't. Do I love it that "authors" like Justin Bieber rake in advances with twice as many zeros as most of the talented, hardworking wordsmiths I know? No, I wish we had a better model for collaborations. Am I holding Real Housewives to the craft standards I expect from a Tom Brokaw? Hell, no. But a ghosted memoir is not the sum of those parts; it's the integrated project that brings peace, healing, and closure to the client, prosperity to the writer, and a pleasant experience to the hungry reader.

My first high-profile ghostwriting client was Lance Armstrong's mother, who was an amazing woman in her own right. This was, of course, long before the fall of the demigod. Lance's feet of clay were still firmly locked onto the pedals of his high-tech racing bicycle, and people all over the world loved him. He was on track for his severalth Tour de France victory, and in the course of the project, Gary and I followed several stages of the Tour de France through the French Alps.

Years later, someone doing an NPR piece about ghostwriting asked me what the most challenging part of my first gig was, and I had to confess it was trying to pee into those rustic hole-in-the-floor out-houses in the French countryside. I could not bring myself to do it. I refrained from drinking and held my water until I was in abject agony and ended up with a kidney infection. No joke. Since I was a child, I've had this shy bladder issue. Really. It's a thing. Shy bladder. Paruresis. Google it before you judge me.

At the end of Le Tour, we were invited to hang out with Robin Williams, Sheryl Crow, and a host of other swanky people on the fin-ish line bleachers in Paris, but it didn't seem necessary to the book, and that kind of thing really isn't my scene. Gary and I opted to stop off in Geneva, where we sat at an outdoor café, drinking wine and eating pizza with potatoes on it while the peloton blazed down the Champs-Élysées on a Jumbotron just up the walking mall. It was one of the loveliest afternoons of my life. I felt that click; I was in exactly the right place with exactly the right person.

I went on to do a number of high-profile memoirs with celebrities in music, movies, television, sports, and politics. These were big books for the publishers, so I ended up working with top-tier editors at major New York publishing houses and great mid-size presses in the US and UK. I welcomed stringent, feet-to-the-fire developmental, structural, line, and copy editing. Every phase was an education unto itself.

I was a little stunned when I received my first editing job offer at a big New York publisher and only a little less stunned when I received the second, but both began with, "Would you be willing to move to New York?" And I wasn't. I liked being out of the crazy lane, pleasantly ensconced in Houston, a beautiful city with baller ballet and opera companies, TexMex food and lazy bayous, and flowers blooming year-round. The massive airport where Gary worked has no shortage of flights to the east and west coasts. It even has a red-eye to Paris, which came in handy on more than one occasion.

Beyond that, the thought of being one with the storied Gatekeepers did not appeal to me at all, because I'd been outside those gates for so much of my career. I was beginning to see the cracks in the foundation of the New York publishing industry model, and I didn't want to be there when it all came crashing down. In 2008, the American economy hit the wall, so in 2009–2010, there was a great bloodletting in the industry. If I'd taken either of those jobs, I would have been out in the cold with a lot of other editors who were more skilled and far more senior than I was.

Instead, I was happily doing ghostwriting gigs, making enough money to fund the time I spent working on my fiction soul projects, which I felt sure would someday, somehow, see the light of day.

Since the arrival of the hummingbird harbingers, I've ghosted more than thirty books—many of them *New York Times* bestsellers. Several have my name on the cover, most others mention me in the acknowledgments, and the rest are a delicious secret, no less satisfying for the fact that someone else got all the glitter.

The ghostwriting schedule tends to be feast and famine, and believe it or not, the feast phases are worse. The money's great, but after several months of eighteen-hour days, my eye starts twitching. During the dry spells, money gets scary, but I'm able to focus on writing fiction and traveling with the Gare Bear, both of which make me happy.

In the course of working my memoir guru mojo for Kristin Chenoweth—who is, for my taste, the most amazing Broadway diva who ever breathed a high note—I made the acquaintance of Aaron Sorkin, who was her significant other at the time, and for some odd reason, he decided that we should be friends. He's one of the most interesting people I've ever met. Generous, kind, whipsaw funny, scary smart, endearingly geeky. I was appalled at the idea of writing scenes for this book, putting dialogue in the mouth of Aaron Sorkin, so I asked him to be his own voice in the book, and he agreed to supply a chapter—which is, of course, a funny and endearing chapter, even though they'd broken up by the time the book was published.

He's a writer's writer and was incredibly generous with his time. Beyond our conversation about the chapter, we had many long conversations about craft, and each one was like a private master class in storytelling and dialogue. He filled in major gaps in my understanding of the world of television and encouraged me to move into screenwriting and script doctoring, which I did, later on.

He called me Casper at first. The friendly ghost, dontcha know. By the time the project wrapped, he was calling me Cyrano, and that made me extremely proud. I called him "Studs Mulligan." I don't remember why.

Mulligan offered to host the final table read of the manuscript at his home on the Fourth of July, which was probably Kristin's only day off so far this millennium. She is the hardest working woman I know in Hollywood and on Broadway. Mulligan lived in an ultra-moderne but not grossly huge home on a hill overlooking LA, the squarest, hippest, whitest, cleanest house I'd ever seen. The sparse bachelor pad furnishings were complimented with typical mega-star knick-knacks, my favorite being a Gibson Les Paul autographed by Amie Mann. The kitchen was stocked with beverages, treats, and a deli-catered lunch.

Out on the patio, I distributed manuscripts to Kristin, her assistant, myself, and Jerusha, who was working as my assistant and would read the entire book to us out loud while we each marked changes on our hard copy. This table read is my final step with every memoir collaboration, and I do it by myself for every novel.

If you take nothing else from this entire book, take this bit of advice:

## READ YOUR FINISHED MANUSCRIPT ALOUD BEFORE YOU PULL THE TRIGGER.

Seriously. Trust me. You will be *schwamazed*. Every flaw leaps out, every strength shines through, and you'll have a totally new understanding of what your words sound like inside the reader's head.

I had a manuscript printed for Mulligan, just in case, but I was relieved when he respectfully withdrew to his office, wanting to give the rest of us the time and space we needed. During the first six hours of reading and notes, he joined us only when invited to hear one particular chapter or another. Kristin, a boundless ball of energy, wanted to blaze on to the end, and even though I'd been working without stop since 4:00 a.m. in order to have the manuscripts ready, I was prepared to accommodate her. We both insisted we were good to go, but Mulligan gently insisted we take a thirty-minute break.

While the girls went for a swim, I went to a chaise in a shady corner and was asleep about three seconds later. After twenty minutes or so, Jerusha woke me up, and I went to take a quick whiz before resuming the read-through.

The nearest of the many bathrooms in Mulligan's house was just off the space age kitchen. I went in and locked the door and found myself utterly unable to pee. Something about the square fixtures, the shininess of the hardware, the whiteness of everything—I don't know. It was that shy bladder thing. Ridiculous! Anyway, I realized I was about to be bare-assed on the john in the home of this iconic writer I'd worshipped since I saw *A Few Good Men*. ("You want me on that wall! You need me on that wall!") I'd been drinking one water bottle after another. For six hours. I seriously needed to pee, but the pee was not happening. I turned on the water in the *Star Trek*-ish sink to see if that would help.

No. Couldn't do it.

I finally decided the best thing for me to do would be to go out and say that I'd forgotten something at my hotel, which was only five minutes away. I'd dash over there, use the modestly middle-class facility, dash back to Mulligan's, and continue the read-through without consuming another drop of liquid. I hitched up my jeans, rinsed my hands, and wiped them on my pants rather than touch the pristine white towels. But when I tried to open the door ...

The door wouldn't open.

I clicked the little space age locky thingy in and out a couple times. No use. I bent down and gandered at the chrome knob. All I saw was my own sheepish face reflecting back at me. I tugged on the mechanism, which was like a skinny little grenade pin, and heard a small click. Breathing a sigh of relief, I turned the knob, and the little lock pin, which probably cost more than my car, plinked onto the floor like a bullet casing.

I heard my daughter's voice in the kitchen, and I hissed her name a few times, but she drifted back out to the lanai, laughing with my client's assistant. I jiggled and toggled and worked at the doorknob for what seemed like a very long time. Then I started laughing. And the more I laughed, the worse I needed to pee. No way I was going to make it back to my hotel even if I were to get the dang door open and sprint for the rental car this very second.

The ridiculousness of it! For crying out loud.

I dropped trou, took care of whiz biz, washed my hands and dried them on the towel hospitably offered for that purpose. I decided that before I swallowed what was left of my dignity and started yelling for help, I'd give the doorknob one more try.

*Click.* It opened as easy as you please.

Back out on the lanai, I set the lock pin on the table next to Mulligan's hand and said, "I broke your house. I'm sorry."

"Oh. It does that. You have to go *crr-chk-a-chkk*." He demonstrated the gesture with sound effects. "Use the one off the music room."

Jerusha read on for Kristin and me while Mulligan went out and fetched Italian food. I read to the table while everyone else ate, then Mulligan read his chapter while I ate. I resumed reading to the end, which left everyone in tears, because Kristin is such a deeply beautiful person, and that shines through in her book. With the task of the table read accomplished, we raised a toast to Kristin and to the book, and Mulligan presented us both with roses.

## WRITING A BOOK IS A BIG DEAL.

I'd gotten used to the bittersweet ache I always felt as I honored that moment alone. I can't describe what it meant to me to have someone recognize what it means to plant a flag on the mountaintop of that last page. This is the first time the homecoming celebration was even close to being in balance with the enormity of the journey.

It's possible, of course, that with all this, Mulligan was just trying to score points with my client, whom he adored—at the time—with schoolboy blue devotion. Whatever his motives, the experience was wonderful for me.

After dinner, we sat around the fire pit, and our lively conversation covered everything from Cyrano de Bergerac to Barack Obama. While the fireworks went off in the city below, Mulligan gave a talk on the little-known history of the Declaration of Independence, and I am tragically geeky enough to think that was the most awesome part of the whole evening.

Before Jerusha and I left, Mulligan repeated his assertion that I should "come over to the dark side" and try screenwriting.

"I would really love to," I said, "but that's not my world. I'm a book person."

But the next morning, I woke up wondering why I'd set such arbitrary, nonsensical boundaries in my life. Ever since I signed my very first book contract, some destructive little part of my ego-averse id had been telling me I was out of my league. It kept singing that old bluegrass song, *"Don't git above yer raisin'…"*

Getting locked in that bathroom was a blessing. It slapped a leash on me just as I was about to take flight, which would have been an idiotic waste of time in the middle of a hardworking day. And it would have reinforced the utterly wrong idea that I could not function on the most basic human level in what was, for that day, my workplace. Nothing about Mulligan's house or Mulligan himself could have possibly been more welcoming. The only thing telling me I didn't belong there was my own insecurity. I don't have time for that. I need to be able to function comfortably wherever my work is. That means being able to use a Porta-Potty at a rock concert or a hole-in-the-ground outhouse in rural France or a Frank Lloyd Wright toiletron in Hollywood as unfussily as I use the loo off my own kitchen (which is, by the way, wallpapered with pages torn from an old copy of my first novel).

When I thought about it that way, I felt that click. Right place. Right time. Right people. I felt it again a few summers later while Jerusha and I were encamped in the Hollywood Hills at the home of a famous director, doctoring a script, and again when we sat together in a dark movie theater, watching our work on the big screen.

## MY WORLD IS WRITING. EVERYWHERE IT TAKES ME IS HOME.

Studying screenwriting—mostly by reading and writing screenplays—has had a huge influence on the way I write novels and memoirs. And thousands of hours spent reading and writing novels and memoirs elevates my screenwriting. The passage between the two is an unlocked door.

**PEOPLE WILL TELL YOU THAT WRITING IS TOO DIFFICULT, THAT IT IS IMPOSSIBLE TO GET YOUR WORK PUBLISHED, THAT YOU MIGHT AS WELL HANG YOURSELF. MEANWHILE, THEY'LL KEEP WRITING AND YOU'LL HAVE HANGED YOURSELF.**

JOHN GARDNER
AUTHOR OF *THE ART OF FICTION*

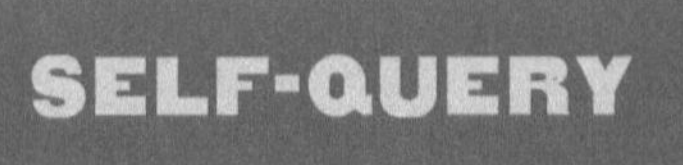



# WHAT'S IN MY WAY?

Reality-check the obstacles between where you are now as a writer and where you'd like to be in five years. Write them down. And then see how they hold up.

Start with the typical issues:

- Time
- Workspace/Technology
- Education

What else ya got?

_______________________________________________

_______________________________________________

_______________________________________________

_______________________________________________

_______________________________________________

Try meditating on each of these with one challenging word: *Really?*

IT IS NOT THE STRONGEST OF THE SPECIES THAT SURVIVES, NOR THE MOST INTELLIGENT THAT SURVIVES. IT IS THE ONE THAT IS THE MOST ADAPTABLE TO CHANGE.

CHARLES DARWIN
AUTHOR OF *THE ORIGIN OF SPECIES*

# 10

# WAIT FOR IT

The basic plot in *The Hurricane Lover* sparked while Gary and I were volunteering with relief efforts in the wake of Hurricane Katrina. Almost a quarter of a million evacuees flooded into shelters in downtown Houston. As I carried water to people in the long FEMA lines outside the Reliant Center, a New Orleans police officer said to me, "This is the greatest thing that ever happened to con artists and media people."

The story hammer hit me full in the head. I stayed up typing all night and went back to the shelter in the morning to carry water, my mind still in unstoppable story gear.

Four weeks later, Hurricane Rita roared toward Houston, causing a massive—and deadly—panic that gridlocked the entire metroplex. We didn't get the worst of the storm, but our power was out for three days. I plugged my laptop into my car charger and kept writing.

When I told my agent I'd started a new novel, he said, "Please, tell me it has nothing to do with hurricanes. I'm so sick of all this hurricane crap on TV."

I haltingly told him that, well, yeah, it did, but … but …

"No," he said flatly. "Let's work on something else."

We did. The DDDSB.

It took me a year or so to get another agent after I was orphaned, and the agent I finally did get wanted to rep me as a ghostwriter only. For her, it was a no-brainer: I was a failure as a novelist and a success as a ghostwriter.

## DO THE MATH.

But a lot happened in the wake of this failure, and three things in particular turned the failure into a gift:

In 2006, over a thousand pages of email to and from Michael Brown and other FEMA officials—from the days leading up to Katrina through the weeks after—were released via the Freedom of Information Act. I inhaled them, sometimes laughing, several times crying. Incorporating the actual text of several of those emails brought an entirely new dimension to the book.

The following year, I ghosted that memoir with the delicious Kristin Chenoweth and met Aaron Sorkin, one of the luckiest perks of my career. He asked for a copy of the *Hurricane Lover* manuscript, which I was thrilled to provide, of course, but not before I tortured myself tweaking until four in the morning. Aaron said he read it, which in Hollywood probably means he skimmed the first fifty pages and had his assistant digest the rest, but that was enough. The surgical story advice and genuine kudos he offered bullet-proofed my belief in that book—and in my ability to write it. Hearing Aaron Sorkin say that you have a great gift for dialogue is the ultimate Califorgasm of validation.

Before we wrapped Kristin's project and parted ways (the two of them eventually parted ways as well), I asked him for a reading list, and his first recommendation was William Goldman's *Adventures in the Screen Trade*, which should be required reading for every novelist. It's filled with laser-specific, right-on advice like: "Enter the story as late as you can." Think about that one with a bike helmet handy, because your mind will be blown when you apply it on a chapter, paragraph, and even grammatical level. Aaron also gave me a stack of his own screenplays, which I've since studied in great detail. Each one is mini-masterclass in itself.

The following summer, Hurricane Ike ripped into the Gulf Coast, laying waste to Galveston and devastating the city of Houston. During the height of the storm, I went outside. Having been brain-deep in storm research off and on for three years, I wasn't about to miss the opportunity to know what it felt and smelled and sounded like—and it was unlike anything I could have imagined.

This time our power was out for over a month, but our wonderful neighbors, George and Toni, snaked a long orange extension cord from their generator to our garage. For almost six weeks, I was able to power the only three things that mattered: the refrigerator, one lamp, and my laptop.

I rewrote the manuscript again, building on the research, incorporating everything I'd experienced during Katrina, Rita, and Ike, and employing screenplay structural philosophy. In the beginning, I thought my objective was to make it more attractive for film option, but as I applied cinematic technique on a scene-by-scene basis—a sentence-by-sentence basis—the transformation was thrilling. At the end of the day, I had a bigger, beefier story with about thirty thousand fewer words.

## CLARITY. BREVITY. FORWARD MOTION.

That conscious weighing of words I'd always leaned toward instinctively, not knowing why it gave me such pleasure, only knowing that it worked when I got it right—now I knew *why* it worked, and I got it right a lot more often. But I could also see how all that discarded material had brought me to this point, revealing what I needed to know about mechanics and motivations in order to cut to the proverbial chase.

Elie Wiesel: "Writing is not like painting where you add. It is not what you put on the canvas that the reader sees. Writing is more like a sculpture where you remove; you eliminate in order to make the work visible. Even those pages you remove somehow remain."

You know the old adage:

## WRITE HOT, EDIT COLD.

The hard part about that is the cooling off periods. That gestation takes time. For me, fiction is an orchard, not a factory. I've ghostwritten books in as little as twenty-eight days, but I have yet to publish a novel that took less than three years to write.

By the time our world had returned to normal with lights, internet, hot water, and a host of other decadences I would never again take for granted, the book felt right. I was a bit stricken to realize that getting rejected on concept by HarperCollins years earlier was the luckiest thing that could have happened to this novel. Now it felt finished. And I knew exactly what I wanted to do with it. After fifteen years in corporate publishing, I decided to indie publish.

*PUT IT BEFORE THEM
BRIEFLY SO THEY WILL
READ IT, CLEARLY SO THEY
WILL APPRECIATE IT,
PICTURESQUELY SO THEY
WILL REMEMBER IT, AND,
ABOVE ALL, ACCURATELY SO
THEY WILL BE GUIDED BY ITS
LIGHT.*

JOSEPH PULITZER
PUBLISHER/ACTIVIST

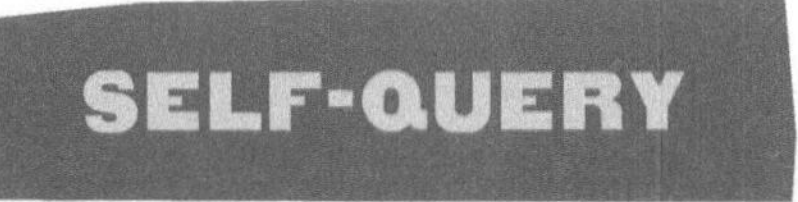


# WHAT DIFFERENCE DOES IT MAKE?

Book deals are not always—or possibly ever—strictly about cash. There are "tangible intangibles," the values of which are constantly changing. It's up to the author to weigh the give and take of book deal. We have more options now than ever before. Before you sign on the dotted line, ask yourself:

- Is this a step forward in my writing career?
- Will I feel good about making changes they're asking for?
- Will I be supported in the launch, or will I have to spend money on PR?
- Will the book support my other revenue streams like speaking, article-writing, or teaching?
- Will I learn from the editor?
- Will I have fun?
- What are the other non-cash benefits of the deal?

Ghostwriters, turn the page for a more detailed way of sussing out the viability of ghostwriting gigs.

# THE GHOSTWRITING GIG-O-MATIC

To be or not to be? That is the question. If you're on the fence about a ghostwriting project, ask the questions, identify issues, and highlight accordingly:

- Green = *Do it!*
- Yellow = *Meh.*
- Blue = *Run, you fool!*
- Magenta = *DANGER, WILL ROBINSON!*

Step back and look at the big picture. Color-coding doesn't lie.
Client:

- Name
- Agent

Project:

- Logline
- Word count
- Deadline

Client's goals/expectations:

- Publishing path (traditional / indie / hybrid)
- Creative process
- Financials
- Personal interaction (hands-on / hands-free)
- Optimal end point
- Acceptable end point
- Other:

Estimated hours:

- Realistic minimum =
- Worst case maximum =
- How might I positively/negatively influence this outcome?

- o Bulletproof against time suck w/ ironclad structure/ outline
  - o Multitask materials
  - o Other
- How might client positively/negatively influence this outcome?
  - o Platform
  - o Temperament
  - o Resources
  - o Other

Possible financial outcomes:

- My ideal deal
  - o Proposal fee
  - o Book fee
  - o Structured deal (floor/ceiling)
  - o Bestseller bonus
  - o Cover credit
- Client is offering
  - o Proposal
  - o Kill fee
  - o Flat fee
  - o Structured deal

How will my time be used?

- Research including interviews and travel = XX%
- Writing and revisions = XX%
- Possible/probable agent/editor/client shenanigans = XX%

What are the potential benefits?

- Short-term active income
- Long-term passive income
- Writing joy factor
- Immersion in fascinating research
- Easy deal/pub contract already set

- Networking/building relationships
- Impact on CV
- Other:

What are the potential negatives?

- Deadline pressure
- Proposal needed
- Uncertainty of payment
- Certainty of payment below project norms
- High-maintenance relationships
- Onerous NDA/draconian contract issues
- Conflict over creative choices
- Other:

How much creative control will I have?

- None / Some / All or most
- I feel [ great/okay/not okay ] with that because:

How does it impact my overall body of work?

- It doesn't, but it might make the world a better place
- Takes time away from my own projects
- This work will stand as proof of my artistic identity.

Am I being totally and objectively realistic about all of the above?

- Sure. No-brainer.
- Probably some Pollyanna at work.
- Why are we having this conversation?

**QTMBA (Questions That Must Be Asked)**

- Is there any reason I might not want this person in my life?
- Is the approaching agent being honest with me?
- Am I ignoring red flags because I want this to happen?
- If this goes pear-shaped:
    - How will it impact my baseline happiness?
    - How will it impact my finances?

- o   How will it impact my career?
- o   Will I feel that I've been acceptably compensated for my time?
- If this goes well:
  - o   Will I feel as satisfied as I would if I'd spent this time writing my own book?
  - o   Will my work help make this a better world?
  - o   Are there factors that might mitigate red flags?
- Am I genuinely excited to do this work?

**ALL THAT YOU TOUCH, YOU CHANGE. ALL THAT YOU CHANGE CHANGES YOU.**

OCTAVIA BUTLER
AUTHOR OF *PARABLE OF THE SOWER*

# 11

# BE THE LUNATIC WHO TAKES OVER THE ASYLUM

When I first started chemo, I got a lot of discouraging comments from my crunchy granola friends. "Chemotherapy is like removing a wart with a blowtorch," was one popular refrain. When I turned down the recommended course of radiation after chemo, I got the B side from my non-granola friends: "Are you crazy? You should be doing exactly what the doctors tell you!"

When I lost my remission a year after finishing chemo, the *I told ya sos* came at me from both sides, which wasn't helpful as I weighed my options, trying to decide how to go forward. Proponents of chemo and radiation were vehemently against "woo woo" or "alternative" treatments like macrobiotic diet, meditation, Tibetan singing bowls, Rolfing and what have you. Holistic medicine proponents railed against the "slash, poison, and burn" methods of conventional surgery, chemo, and radiation. Neither the polarization nor the pejorative terms were helpful to me, the person fighting for her life.

The consulting oncologist was adamant that I should do the radiation. Standard therapy at M.D. Anderson Cancer Center—arguably the world's best place to be treated for lymphoma—automatically included radiation and bone marrow transplant. But Ro was in private practice by this time, and to her credit, there was room in her belief system for both science and spirituality. She did gently insist that, whatever I decided to do, I had to come in for regular blood work and continue getting scanned from jaw to vajayjay every four weeks.

Ultimately, I did a ton of homework and designed a treatment plan that worked for me, my belief system, and my family's needs, with consideration for my best statistical odds of survival. I turned down the bone marrow transplant, but I continued the scans. I went to a shaman, became vegetarian, meditated, and, yes, I had Tibetan singing bowl therapy. Don't knock it till you've tried it.

I also rewrote the vocabulary—in my own head and in conversation—making sure that people around me were speaking the same language. It wasn't "alternative" medicine, implying either/or, it was "complementary" therapy, a customized combo platter. I can't tell you this is the right way to treat lymphoma; I wouldn't presume to tell anyone what they should or shouldn't do. All I can say is:

## THE ODDS WERE OVERWHELMINGLY NOT IN MY FAVOR. AND I AM STILL HERE.

My approach to publishing is exactly the same.

When I first started talking about indie publishing, I was resoundingly squashed from every direction. My agent was understandably concerned that self-publishing would brand me as someone who wasn't publishable. Almost a dozen books into my career, I wouldn't be a wannabe; I'd be a reject. I wouldn't be the girl who didn't get asked to the prom; I'd be the girl who got asked to the prom by the quarterback, broke a heel, got her period, and ended up like *Carrie*, doused in a bucket of critical pig blood.

On the flip side, all we heard rising to the front of the self-publishing world were vociferous, uninformed tirades against the vagaries of the industry, the evil intent of agents and the shortsightedness of whoever signed the rejection letter. It was off-putting, untrue, and amateurish. I didn't want to be part of that conversation.

But as Dorothy Parker said:

## "I DON'T HAVE TO ATTEND EVERY ARGUMENT I'M INVITED TO."

My priorities haven't changed since chemo—my life, my belief system, and my family's needs, in balance with my best statistical odds of survival—and believe me, the odds of long-term survival in publishing are even worse than they are with a virulent blood cancer.

As fate would have it, I still owned the digital rights to *Bald in the Land of Big Hair*. Back in 2000, when the contract was being forged, there was some chatter about Lifetime optioning the movie rights. My longevity was still a big question mark in our lives, and Gary and I felt that a movie—especially one in which I had no creative say or script approval—could turn out to be a bad thing for our kids if I wasn't around anymore. It killed us to turn down the money, but it was the right thing to do, so I retained my electronic rights.

Fast-forward ten years.

Much to my surprise, I was still alive, the digital publishing revolution was in full swing, and I owned the ebook rights to this memoir that had gone much further than I ever imagined it would. The paperback was still in print at HarperCollins. They were cool with my publishing the ebook, realizing that a new surge of ebook sales would spur paperback sales and generally increase my value as an author. They still owned a piece of me.

*Crazy For Trying* and *Sugarland* had both been out of print for years. After some wrangling, I got all the rights back. Bringing them out of the vault and sharing them with thousands of new readers took me back to that time when the writing process was intensely naked and emotionally fraught, a perilous but thrilling journey, word by word.

I felt that Tom Robbins writing buzz he describes writing as: an extreme state of being next to madness.

# "YOU SHOULD ALWAYS WRITE WITH AN ERECTION. EVEN IF YOU'RE A WOMAN."

I'd almost forgotten what that felt like. It was painful to realize the extent to which I had allowed a modicum of publishing success to erode my creative autonomy, which is key to the unalloyed joy of writing. As a writer, I wasn't about to give that up again, and as a reader, I wondered what I'd been missing as so many other authors went through the same hypnotic state I'd just awakened from.

Years of ghostwriting and editing reverse-engineered the way I read; I started recognizing the editorial handprints on the books I read for pleasure, and as the publishing industry became more pressured financially, those handprints started looking more like strangleholds. These days, much of the fiction coming out of New York feels to me, as a reader, over-processed and creatively constipated. The talent and style of the author is there, but it's been airbrushed, spray-tanned, and boob-jobbed. It sometimes has that sad, self-deluded trout pout you see on women who've forgotten how to kiss with their own collagen-free lips.

With my first Kindle, my reading life began to breathe again. First, all those free and cheap classics—heaven! Then I poked around the web for authors who'd fallen from grace for one reason or another and were going it alone after leaving—or being thrown out of—their traditional publishing homes. I renewed friendships with many of my favorite books from the past and discovered a few debut gems that completely rewrote my prejudiced view of self-publishing, which—yes, I'll admit it—I had always seen as synonymous with "amateur crap."

Candidly, there is a lot of amateur crap in the self-publishing mosh pit, but in 2011, seven of my ten favorite novels were indie pubbed, delivered directly from the authors' lips to my Kindle without being sanitized for my protection. With my old woodchipper reading verve, I consumed novels by top drawer literary craftspeople. I discovered that artists with proven publishing chops were jumping the turnstile and doing their best work ever as indies. I didn't have to make an extraordinary effort to find women authors; they were thriving in the indie world.

While my kids were growing up, I ingrained in them Polonius's advice to Laertes in *Hamlet*:

"This above all: To thine own self be true."

"Be true," I'd call as they headed out to the school bus and later on to their cars. After they left home, I had the words tattooed on my back with a portrait of William Shakespeare.

## BE TRUE.

It's so much simpler and so much harder than it sounds, especially when you want something so damn bad that the compromises are palatable. At least, they seem to be. For a while.

I've enjoyed all the wonderful things aspiring authors hope they'll get out of the publishing process. Validation. Money. The affirmation of critical petting and the education of critical smackdown. My name on the cover of a book. My books on the bestseller lists. I'm grateful. Profoundly grateful. Forehead to the floor, teary-eyed, praise God from whom all blessings flow grateful. But I've "been to the puppet show and seen the strings," as they say.

Over the years, I watched fiction acquisitions become increasingly narrow, while nonfiction acquisitions became obsessed with celebrity. Creative writing majors were pumped out of grad school with not a clue about how to make a living writing, creatively or otherwise. For all the handwringing about the fate of booksellers, I heard very little concern for those of us who've dedicated our lives to the creation of books. It never seemed to occur to anyone that the health of literary culture might be maybe-possibly-kinda related to the care and feeding of authors.

Having learned what an author gets and gives up in the old-school publishing system, I was fully aware of what I'd get and give up if I went indie. There will always be compromises. In this case, it was worth it.

So the story I wanted to tell is out there, and I'm back where I started, personally delivering my stories directly into the hands of readers. I feel like I've come full circle. On roller skates.

Most writers, I'm sure, share my big picture goals: the greatest possible joy and the biggest possible paycheck. I'm willing to sacrifice some income for joy and sacrifice some joy for income, but the goal is to get a healthy balance of the two. For me, that means a hybridized approach, just like it did in chemo.

Dedication to craft hasn't exactly been a hallmark in the emerging mosh pit of self-publishing, but it's not always the hallmark in corporate publishing either. Crap is sometimes king in either world. In both worlds, there's an agonizingly thin tier of people who get struck by lightning and make it really big. Under that tier, a moderate strata of folks like myself make a good living, for which we are grateful. Then there's the other 96 percent of writers: a roiling, frustrated, passionate, and increasingly empowered population of people who are mad as hell and not taking it anymore.

Democratization is either terrifying or a Godsend, depending on your perspective and your willingness to roll with the changes. As the ebook revolution unfolds and the two worlds come together in a way that benefits all of us—authors, readers, agents, publishers, booksellers, and the industry as a whole—we need rhetoric that's respectful of the choices being made by others, honest about who we want to be as writers, and realistic about financial expectations.

I wouldn't presume to tell you what you should or shouldn't do. All I can say is, the odds were overwhelmingly not in my favor, and I am still here.

The vocabulary that works for me (for now) includes "indie publishing," which celebrates the reclaiming of my creative autonomy, as opposed to "self-publishing," which implies that I do it all myself. One of the responsibilities of indie publishing—arguably the most challenging—is the protection of our creative energy and writing time.

The little red hen do-it-myself mentality doesn't serve writers well.

I've taken the trouble to learn how to do everything myself, but I bring in help for editing, design, and technology.

I say "corporate publishing" when I refer to the business model in action at the big houses like HarperCollins and Penguin Random House, because "traditional" implies a values system. It always struck me as odd that state-of-the-art molecular scans and chemo were called "traditional therapies," while ancient Chinese tinctures were "new age." It makes even less sense to say that Justin Bieber's ghostwritten memoir is "traditionally published," but a diligently crafted novel by an indie Tolstoy scholar is not.

Traditional publishing isn't about a big house brand; it's about artistic integrity, zeal for writing, respect for careful editing, thoughtful presentation. All those are possible in the brave new world of indie publishing, which is becoming a high ground for craft-conscious, creatively daring authors.

That said, it behooves us to remember that old-school publishing professionals did learn a thing or two over the past five hundred years.

## GLITTER DOESN'T STICK. POWERFUL STORIES DO.

*IT IS AWFULLY IMPORTANT
TO KNOW WHAT IS AND IS
NOT YOUR BUSINESS.*

GERTRUDE STEIN
FROM "WHAT IS ENGLISH LITERATURE?"

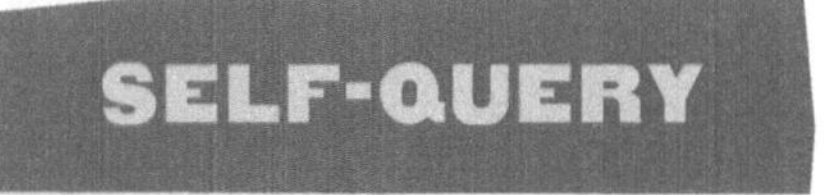



# WHOSE LIFE IS IT ANYWAY?

Thinking of your own story—the writer in search of self—or the story you're trying to tell: Who is the protagonist? It seems like a no-brainer, but it's shockingly easy for secondary characters to hijack the story, which weakens the protagonist. The story is not about the rabbit; it's about Alice experiencing the rabbit hole.

Who is the protagonist in your story?

How do we know the truth of who the protagonist really is?

How do the protagonist's priorities guide plot points?

# 12

# KEEP REELING
# AND WRITHING

**T**ectonic shifts continue to rock and roll the publishing industry. In my little corner of the book universe, the learning curve still looks a lot like a roller coaster, but learn we do, white-knuckles notwithstanding.

The London Book Fair was definitely the highpoint of that year for me; 2012 turned out to be one of the toughest years of my life, personally and professionally. I was chained to a ghostwriting client from hell, and as I exhausted myself trying to keep the publishing plates spinning, I became increasingly aware that something was deeply, terribly wrong with my mom.

My mother, author and historian Lois Lonnquist, who had retired from her career as a newspaper editor, had always been fiercely independent, intensely private, and always—always—in control. Of everything.

Every. Thing.

Which is why she was an early adopter of self-publishing. Assisted by my father, who's been an early adopter of technology since television was the next big thing, she released *Fifty Cents an Hour*, a meticulously researched history of the Montana boom towns surrounding Fort Peck Dam, a WPA project featured in the very first issue of *Life Magazine*. Niche nonfiction of this sort, when it's done well, thrives in the self-publishing environment. It was quickly recognized that Mom was the foremost authority on the history of the building of the dam, which the *Life* article had gotten spectacularly wrong.

On a mission to set the record straight, Mom dedicated several years to the project, trekking to cemeteries and libraries and microfiche dungeons all over the state, interviewing the rapidly vanishing denizens of the boom towns—mostly ghost towns now—and confirming the identity of every man who'd been killed during the building of the dam. (If you're interested in learning more about a fascinating bit of Americana, I encourage you to read *Fifty Cents an Hour* or check out the PBS documentary *Fort Peck Dam,* in which she's featured.)

Flash forward to 2012.

Jerusha and I arrived at my parents' home in Montana early that summer to find that my brilliant mother had become a painfully thin shadow of herself. She had Alzheimer's and had been given a literally mind-blowing dose of the wrong drug. The downward spiral was swift and terrifying. Suddenly, she was living in a wraith-world where nightmares and memories mingled, whispering and plotting at the edges of a baffling surreality.

Books, papers, and random objects in her office kept moving around, disappearing, transforming infuriatingly. She was confronted with only two possible explanations: either she was losing her mind or strangers were lurking in the basement, stealing from her and cluttering her workspace with inexplicable midden. For my mother, the latter option was the less terrifying, and she'd embraced it with increasing paranoia. In varying states of rant, she muttered and agonized about "Nellie" and other unwelcome squatters, obsessively packing and bundling things, trying to "organize" old papers, clip files, and photos. My mother's house had always been neat as a proverbial pin. That summer, Jerusha and I arrived to find something that looked like an episode of *Hoarders.*

My father was struggling to rise to the occasion and care for her at their home in Montana, but it was agreed that Mom and Dad should fly to my sister's in Florida where Dad could take a break and Mom could be evaluated by a geriatric specialist.

On the morning they were to depart, her purse, ID, and passport were nowhere to be found. Her worst nightmares came true as Jerusha and I—two strangers, as far as Mom was concerned—ransacked her things, searching for her wallet. She was beside herself, beyond distraught, begging us to leave her house and let her be. In desperation, I called my nephew who works for the TSA in Denver and asked, "Is there any way I can put your grandma on an airplane without her ID?"

"Maybe," he said. "It's a small town. Grandpa's got his ID, so come up with whatever you can that has both her name and his."

"Easy. Checkbook."

"But you need something that has her name and a photo of her. To prove that it's her."

An hour later, my parents stepped up to a special services podium at the airport, and Mom presented the TSA agent with the irrefutable proof of who she is, the avatar of her real self: her book.

In one of those lightning bolt moments, I saw with perfect clarity what my work means to me.

It *is* me.

It's the manifestation of myself that will survive whatever phantoms or cancer or brain death lurk in my future. And frankly, compared to those scenarios, the chatter and crap of the publishing industry is not the gold standard for scary.

My work is the synthesis of everything I've learned in my first half-century, an education that bears an uncanny resemblance to the undersea curriculum of Lewis Carroll's Mock Turtle: "Reeling and writhing, of course, and the different branches of arithmetic—ambition, distraction, uglification and derision."

By the end of the summer, I had extracted myself from the ill-fated ghost gig, sacrificing the income, welcoming the priceless peace that replaced it. I revised and published a mystery novel under my nom de plume, the product of a three-month pure pleasure-reading binge followed by a three-month pure pleasure-writing binge—the most fun I've ever had writing a book. Ever.

In the fall, I landed a dream ghost gig with a performing artist I've admired since I was a teen, and she was a joy to work with. Unfortunately, I also had a pretty jolting cancer scare that resulted in a radical hysterectomy. Afterward, I crawled in bed and read for six weeks, emotionally and physically beaten down.

Reading has been my refuge since I was a child.

## WHEN THE GOING GETS TOUGH, READING IS BOTH AN ANCHOR TO SANITY AND AN ESCAPE FROM REALITY.

So often the right book will speak to me at the right moment, and the book that spoke to me in that moment was David Mitchell's *Cloud Atlas*. I was curious when I started and weeping when I finished. In between, I was taken heart and soul. Resonating in the background were some of my favorite reading experiences: The majesty and moral character of Melville's *Moby Dick*. The gimlet eye and heartbreaking hindsight of Michener's *Hawaii*. The rich, musical ethos of Elise Blackwell's *An Unfinished Score*. The hardboiled cunning of Elmore Leonard's *Out of Sight*. The chilling resonance of George Orwell's *1984*. The bleak dystopian vision of Cormack McCarthy's *The Road*.

Each of the six worlds in *Cloud Atlas* vividly awakened sense memories, books, music, movies, conversations, experiences. The nesting doll metaphor is apt for the structure of the novel itself but doesn't talk about the air in between, where a willing reader will feel his/her own personal past and future. This is one of those rare books capable of drawing you in on that level.

The writing craft is fine, and I mean *fine* fine, as in particularly, specifically, exquisitely made. The range and depth of voices is spectacular; I experienced only a few moments of dialogue fatigue. The storytelling is entertaining and pace-conscious with philosophizing that feels more conversational than preachy. The concept is brilliant without being overworked or parlor-tricky. The infrastructure of the story is a balls-out astonishing accomplishment. All of which is to say, it's one of those books that functions as a masterclass on how to be a better writer.

Brenda Ueland:

## "WRITING IS NOT A PERFORMANCE BUT A GENEROSITY."

I believe we must be equally generous as readers, and I think that goes beyond an investment of money or time; I think it's about reading as the breathing in of words, an equal exchange of inhalation and exhalation.

## READING IS OXYGEN FOR THE WRITING BRAIN.

This is something my mother knew well. My earliest memories are of reading. Going to the library with Mom after we dropped the big kids off at school. Lying on my back beneath a card table that functioned as her office, reading a book with the *clack-ack-ack-ack-ack-TING!* of her typewriter over my head. When I wanted to see a movie that was perhaps also a bit over my head, she made me earn it by reading the book first, which is how I came to love *Gone with the Wind*, *Hawaii*, and *Jaws*. It's also how my son came to love *Jurassic Park* and *Starship Troopers*.

Since my mother died, it's the book conversations I miss most. We had a vibrant writerly discourse, and I haven't yet figured out how to write about the period of time when Alzheimer's had taken her ability to think in words. We were forced to transcend our dependence on language, letting go of the grammar and syntax that had filled both our lives, allowing ourselves to simply be together, a heartbreaking and beautiful experience.

To be honest, I had tried to read *Cloud Atlas* a few years earlier and couldn't get into it. I didn't have time for it because I didn't make time for it. Happily, it called to me at a rare moment when I was quiet enough to receive it, and I'll always be grateful for that.

In the final chapter, Adam—with whom, appropriately, we began the journey—takes us to its resolution, forcing us to despair at the utter darkness at the core of humankind, then showing us a redeeming beam of light.

Reflecting on all this and thinking of his son, Adam says:

> **"A LIFE SPENT SHAPING A WORLD I WANT JACKSON TO INHERIT, NOT ONE I FEAR HE SHALL INHERIT; THIS IS A LIFE WORTH LIVING."**

The story had already evoked in my own mind that same thought about the world my children live in now: how we create our culture with every choice we make. As the protagonist translated his good intentions into a pragmatic plan of action, I could see myself doing the same. As flaky as this sounds, I felt a sort of rebirth—as a writer and a daughter and a mother—in this story of transmigrating souls.

"Lord, I hope it's not just painkillers talking," I said to Gary. Because I wanted to take that better self with me into the future.

And I will. I already have in ways I don't even understand.

And I'll bet you have, too.

When *Bald in the Land of Big Hair* was originally published by HarperCollins in 2001, I had no reason to expect that this funny little book by a nobody novelist would take on a quietly powerful life of its own. During its first year, *BLBH* was translated and published around the world, condensed by *Reader's Digest*, excerpted in *Good Housekeeping*, and featured in a special on Oprah's new TV channel. Later, it was adapted for an off-Broadway touring show, and in 2011, a tenth anniversary edition was published with a lovely foreword by

Elizabeth Berg. This book put my name on the bestseller lists for the first time, launched a robust public speaking side gig, and opened the door for my unexpected career as a ghostwriter and memoir guru.

All this was tremendously rewarding, and I'm grateful. An intensely personal memoir takes a lot out of a person; there's a cost to the author and her family. This book was the realization of the promise in Ecclesiastes:

## CAST YOUR BREAD UPON THE WATER; IN TIME, IT WILL RETURN A HUNDREDFOLD.

For me, the greatest gift has been twenty-plus years of rich correspondence and chance encounters with readers.

About five years after *Bald in the Land of Big Hair* was published, I received a long, heart-wrenching email from a Wall Street executive whose daughter, like me, was diagnosed with lymphoma as a young mom. He told me someone had given her an autographed copy of my book. As she struggled through a grueling year of chemo, she'd read it several times and copied bits and quotes from it on Post-it notes that peppered her bathroom mirror, bulletin boards, and refrigerator.

"She wanted to talk to me about what she was going through," he said, "but I wanted to keep up that damn stupid positive attitude."

Frustrated, she'd told him, "If you ever want to know what it was really like, read this book."

She always took it with her when she checked into the hospital, so she had it with her when she began losing ground and slipped into an end stage haze. The man pulled his chair close to the bed and read the whole book to his daughter during the long last night of her life. In the morning, he wrote to me: "They say it'll be another hour or two."

He said he felt compelled to email me because he'd missed his opportunity to talk to her about what she was going through, but now he felt as though he'd laughed and cried with her, that he'd shared in her journey, and that on some level, she knew, because she knew he would eventually read this book.

"Thank you," he said, "for giving me a way to reach her."

It was one of the most precious moments of my writing life.

A few years later, I spoke at a large survivorship event and was signing books afterward, doing my best to hug and listen to each person in the long line but feeling very weary after a long day of travel and workshops. A woman came forward with a hardcover first-edition copy of BLBH. The binding was broken, the dust jacket tattered and coffee-stained, and leafing through the dogeared pages, I could see that the well-worn book had been passed from that original reader to a sister, to a friend, to a daughter, to a book club mate, to a neighbor, to a chemo buddy—one woman after another—each adding notes and highlights in a kaleidoscope of colored pencils, inks, highlighters, and sticky notes.

## THE BOOK HAD BECOME A CONVERSATION.

Opening the book to the title page, I saw that I had already signed it back in 2001: *To my sister in survivorship—shalom and joy, Joni Rodgers*

I thought of the stockbroker's daughter, how she and I, together, had found the language to get past her father's stiff upper lip and allow him to let her go. This couldn't possibly be hers; of course, I knew the vanishingly small odds of that. But in a rush came the realization that this book was one of thousands. There were others, each with its own chorus of voices chiming in with love and support for one another, sharing hopes and fears, creating a sacred space for laughter and tears. They were out there all along; I just didn't know it.

Not gonna lie. I cried.

Oh, how I wish I could have put that gorgeously dilapidated volume in a shadowbox in my office! But it wasn't mine to keep. When I wrote this book, I made the choice to share my story, and with that choice comes the understanding that writers have no control over how or where our words will land—ample reason to choose those words with care.

I launched this little paper sailboat into the stream of consciousness more than two decades ago. Readers are the wind and water that carried it around the world, beyond time, and back to me. It was a profound privilege to hold the proof of that in my hands, a far more meaningful metric for "success" than any bestseller list or bank deposit.

Next to the hurried autograph of the hopeful young author, I added a brief note from my older, wiser self and sent my story on its way.

It belongs to you now.

May it bring you peace.

**MY WISH FOR YOU IS THAT YOU HAVE A NEVER-ENDING SERIES OF DREAMS AND THE FURIOUS DESIRE TO REALIZE A FEW OF THEM.**

JACQUES BREL
FROM THE POEM "OUR DEEPEST FEAR"

# ACKNOWLEDGMENTS

In 2022, I independently republished six books from my backlist:

*Crazy for Trying: 25th Anniversary Author's Cut*

*The Hurricane Lover: 10th Anniversary Edition*

*Bald in the Land of Big Hair: 20th Anniversary Ebook*

*Sugarland*

*Kill Smartie Breedlove*

*Boxing the Octopus: The Worst Way to Become an Almost Famous Author & the Best Advice I Got While Doing It*

This wouldn't have been possible without the stellar team assembled by Reading List Editorial. Special thanks to project manager Salvatore Borriello for his patience, wisdom, and industry expertise; to Lindsey Alexander for her keen insight and enormous kindness; to Kapo Ng for the brilliant reimagining of the cover designs; and to Sharon, Lauren, and the team at BookSavvy PR for busting out the hustle. My assistant Patty Lewis Lott is the divine sparkplug that powers this whole rodeo, and my agent Cindi Davis-Andress continues to work miracles on my behalf—two life-changing partnerships for which I'm grateful every day.

www.ingramcontent.com/pod-product-compliance
Lightning Source LLC
Chambersburg PA
CBHW051448130726
47987CB00005B/2240